100 THINGS TO DO IN DOOR COUNTY BEFORE YOU DIE

On the docks in Egg Harbor

100 THINGS TO DO IN DOOR COUNTY BEFORE YOU DIE

TAMARA GAUMOND AND JEAN O'BRIEN GIBBONS

REEDY PRESS

Reedy Press
PO Box 5131
St. Louis, MO 63139, USA
reedypress.com

Library of Congress Control Number: 2024949024

ISBN: 9781681065243

Design by Jill Halpin

Cover photo courtesy of Jean O'Brien Gibbons

Unless otherwise noted, all photos are courtesy of Jean O'Brien Gibbons or believed to be in the public domain.

Printed in the United States of America
25 26 27 28 29 5 4 3 2

DEDICATION

To Olivia and Tim for the fun times we have and the joy you bring. – Tamara

To my mom and dad for "discovering" Door County almost 50 years ago. – Jean

CONTENTS

Music and Entertainment

Sports and Recreation

Culture and History

Shopping and Fashion

ACKNOWLEDGMENTS

A heartfelt thanks to my dear friend Jean O'Brien Gibbons for collaborating with me on this book and for all the fun we've had in Door County over the years. I am also deeply grateful to my kids, extended family, and many friends who have been part of my Door County experience and who have supported me in my writing endeavors.

–Tamara

Thanks to my husband for falling in love with Door County, and to my two daughters and the generations of O'Brien, Gibbons, Ward, Ferruzzi, and Olson family members for years of wonderful Door County memories. And thanks to Tamara Gaumond for her loyal friendship and her gift of capturing the spirit of each of the 100 things with her skillful and entertaining writing.

– Jean

Together, we'd like to thank Reedy Press for the opportunity to include Door County in the *100 Things* family of books.

And of course, we are very grateful for Door County, its people, businesses, and organizations as well as its wonderment and natural beauty. Thank you for continuing to fill our lives with awe, inspiration, and joy.

PREFACE

Welcome to Door County!

If you are not familiar with Door County, you are in for a surprise. Often dubbed "the Cape Cod of the Midwest," Door County is the narrow peninsula jutting into Lake Michigan on the northeast coast of Wisconsin. The county boasts miles of shoreline, picturesque villages, and nautical flair. It was named after Death's Door, the passage of water separating the top of the peninsula and Washington Island that is associated with tales shared by early explorers of rough waters and shipwrecks.

The peninsula is only about 18 miles at its widest point, less than two miles wide at its northernmost point, and about 42 miles long from the shipping channel in Sturgeon Bay to the Washington Island Ferry port. Part of the Niagara Escarpment, Door County features impressive rocky bluffs along its shoreline as well as forests and inland waterways. And Wisconsin is an agricultural state, so the peninsula contains fields, orchards, and vineyards.

Enough about the geography; let's get to the fun stuff! Door County has pristine beaches; lighthouses; natural wonders; sprawling state and county parks; a robust art scene including galleries, theater, and live music; four-season sporting opportunities; unique and notable restaurants; breweries and wineries; loads of shopping; rich history and culture; and awesome kids' activities. Whew!

With so much to do in Door County, capturing a list of 100 things was daunting. Everyone's perfect Door County experience is unique, and we sought to have the list truly reflect our favorites while still being comprehensive. Unfortunately, we couldn't include everything. But we hope this book will give newbies an exciting and thorough starting point and seasoned Door County enthusiasts a nudge to try something new. We are certain you will fall in love with this magical place. But remember, "Shhhhhh," it just might be one of the best-kept secrets in the Midwest.

One of many picturesque Door County harbors

Dining alfresco at Stone's Throw Winery

FOOD AND DRINK

1

ENJOY THE SHOW
AT A DOOR COUNTY FISH BOIL

Sure, there's tender whitefish, but the main event at a Door County fish boil is the theatrics. Grab a cold beverage, sit back, and be regaled by a boil master explaining the history and process of a fish boil, with possibly a few tall tales mixed in. Fish boils are a gift from Door County's Scandinavian heritage and historically were an efficient way to feed large groups of hungry lumberjacks and fishermen.

Taking center stage is a large cauldron on an open fire. A boatload of salt is added to the water, which is then brought to a boil. Potatoes and onions are added, followed by whitefish.

The show's climax is the boilover. Kerosene is tossed on the whole caboodle, creating a startling, heat-emitting, "holy cow"–inducing ball of fire. (Don't try this at home folks!). The tender whitefish, potatoes, and onions are then served along with melted butter, coleslaw, bread, and a piece of cherry pie.

FISH BOIL OPTIONS

We couldn't tease you with the description of a fish boil and not offer a few favorite restaurants offering the delicious and entertaining dining experience.

White Gull Inn

4225 Main St., Fish Creek, 920-868-3517
whitegullinn.com

Pelletier's Restaurant & Fish Boil

4199 Main St., Fish Creek, 920-868-3313
doorcountyfishboil.com

Old Post Office Restaurant

10040 Water St., Ephraim, 920-854-4034
oldpostoffice-doorcounty.com

Waterfront Mary's Bar & Grill

3662 N Duluth Ave., Sturgeon Bay, 920-743-3690
waterfrontmarysbarandgrill.com

Island Fever Rum Bar & Grill

6301 WI-57, Jacksonport, 920-823-2700
islandfeverrumbarandgrill.com

2

HOIST AN ALE
AT SHIPWRECKED

Seafarers and landlubbers alike will enjoy taking a break from their Door County adventure with a bite or a pint at Shipwrecked Brew Pub. Hoist a Captains Copper Ale while enjoying a spot on the popular patio in the center of Egg Harbor.

This nautical-themed brewery and restaurant not only serves classic pub grub such as fish fry, chili, and cleverly named burgers (like the Kraken and the Jolly Roger) but boasts 100 percent handcrafted Door County beers.

The original restaurant burned to the ground in 2017 much to the distress of Door County fans. To everyone's collective relief, a cool new building now stands in its place. But don't be deceived by its newness. Shipwrecked brings a whale of a history and a shipload of lore to the peninsula, including being a retreat for Al Capone and being haunted by a number of ghosts (or at least ghostly stories).

7791 WI-42, Egg Harbor, 920-868-2767
shipwreckedmicrobrew.com

3

ELEVATE YOUR WINE TASTING
AT STONE'S THROW WINERY

You'll think you're in Napa (or even the south of France) when you arrive at Stone's Throw Winery. Stone's Throw exudes a wine-country feeling: the understated elegance of unique cuisine and fine wine set against an agrarian landscape. The centerpiece of the grounds is the building that houses the tasting room and wine bar, a modern structure that rises out of the rustic stone foundation of an existing barn. Lush gardens, outdoor seating, and bocce ball courts add to the ambiance.

More than just a cool tasting room, Stone's Throw was built on the concept of using grapes from California vineyards to create outstanding wine in Door County. The result is an award-winning winery that has been featured in foodie, wine, and business magazines. So, wine lovers, rejoice! Stop by the tasting room and sample a Big Mouth Red or enjoy Tuscan-inspired "stuzzichini" (tapas) dining at Vino! Vino! Wine Bar.

3382 County E, Baileys Harbor, 920-839-9660
stonesthrowwinery.com

EAT SWEDISH AND PEEP GOATS
AT AL JOHNSON'S

Door County has a strong Scandinavian heritage, and nowhere will you feel more Scandi than at Al Johnson's. The food, hygge, goats (yes, goats!), shopping, and Swedish cocktails are all here.

The restaurant is known for its Swedish pancakes. Get yours with a side of lingonberries or Swedish meatballs. Lunch features sandwiches, burgers, and seafood. Or pull up a barstool at Stabbur, a water-facing, family-friendly beer garden. Swedish-themed dishes like Swedish Shrimp Roll can be washed down with a Thor's Hammer or Stockholm Cooler.

But wait! There's more. Let's talk about the goats! The restaurant has a sod roof with goats grazing on it. Yes, they are on the roof! Watch them on the Al Johnson's website goat cams!

10698 N Bay Shore Drive, Sister Bay, 920-854-2626
aljohnsons.com

TIP

If you are in Door County in early June, don't miss the annual Roofing of the Goats festival. The goats parade through town to their lofty perch, and the festival includes live music, food and drink, kids' games, and a Swedish pancake-eating contest.

5

TOUR DE CHEESE CURD

Wisconsin is known for cheese, and Wisconsinites are affectionately known as cheeseheads. A popular cheesy product is a little nugget called a cheese curd, basically a by-product of the cheese-making process and made from curdled milk. While that may sound gross, cheese curds are delicious little balls of chewy cheese that make your teeth squeak. But to add to the delightful decadence and ensure that they taste great with a cold beer, our Wisconsin friends drop them in batter, deep-fry them, and serve them with various dipping sauces!

You will find this Wisconsin delicacy on almost every menu across Door County, and they are prepared differently from place to place. So set your healthy eating aspirations aside and embark on a quest to find the best Door County cheese curd.

For a great cheese curd appetizer, check out the Cowabunga Curds at the Thirsty Cow Taphouse, and for some yummy cheese curds to take home, visit Renard's!

The Thirsty Cow Taphouse
7899 County A, Baileys Harbor, 920-839-9991
thethirstycowtaphouse.com

Renard's Cheese
2189 County DK, Sturgeon Bay, 920-825-7272
renardscheese.co

6

EXPLORE CRAFT BEERS
AT DOOR COUNTY BREWING AND PEACH BARN BREWERY

Exploring regional craft beers? Make sure your travels include these two popular breweries.

Door County Brewing features outstanding craft beers brewed on premises. To add to the fun, enjoy your brew with live music in their taproom and music hall. This cool building has a farm/mining/industrial feel, built with reclaimed wood and bricks. The open and airy hall features a lengthy bar with a joyfully large number of beer tappers delivering brews from their current beer list and their Milwaukee-based sister brewery, Hacienda Beer Co. The grounds include an outdoor beer garden and DCBC Eats for grabbing some sustenance to accompany your Vacationland IPA.

For an impressive selection of unique craft brews (with clever names) make a stop at Peach Barn Farmhouse & Brewery. Kick back in their modern and relaxed Peach Barn bar or their outdoor lounge seating, sample a craft brew, or catch a live music performance. (Also, don't forget to pick up some peaches!)

Door County Brewing Co.
Taproom, DCBC Eats, & Music Hall
8099 WI-57, Baileys Harbor, 920-239-8181
doorcountybrewingco.com

Peach Barn Farmhouse & Brewery
2450 South Bay Shore Dr., Sister Bay
peachbarnbrewing.com

7

STEP BACK IN TIME
AT WILSON'S RESTAURANT AND ICE CREAM PARLOR

Everyone has their own favorite Door County destinations. For many families, no trip to Door County is complete without a visit to Wilson's Restaurant and Ice Cream Parlor. With its cheery red-and-white-striped awnings, flower boxes, and large welcoming porch, Wilson's has been entertaining families from the heart of Ephraim since the turn of the century . . . not the last turn of the century but the one before that.

This restaurant has all the old-timey feels of a classic soda fountain and ice cream parlor. Top off your burger and fries with a frosty mug of root beer and put aside your earbuds to appreciate the good old days with toe-tappers delivered from a classic jukebox.

Of course, Wilson's is probably best known for its ice cream! Grab a cone, find a spot across the street on the water's edge of Eagle Harbor, and watch the sunset.

9990 Water St., Ephraim, 920-854-2041
wilsonsicecream.com

INDULGE IN SEAFOOD
AT HARBOR FISH MARKET AND LURE

Only 18 miles separate Lake Michigan and Green Bay at the peninsula's widest point. With all that water (and boats, and nautical lore, and lighthouses), you are going to crave seafood!

For outstanding seafood, including a traditional New England lobster boil, visit the Harbor Fish Market & Grille in Baileys Harbor. Located in an early-1900s historic building, the fish market was once the tallest building in Door County. The large front porch, relaxed interior, and seafood selection give the experience a hearty New England vibe.

Lure in Sister Bay is a casually elegant seafood-themed restaurant occupying a former Catholic church in a garden setting. The building's original identity is obvious at night when the steeple at the back of the building is lit up. Lure has an upscale menu of sophisticated, locally sourced seafood and steak dinners as well as small plates and sushi.

Harbor Fish Market & Grille
8080 WI-57, Baileys Harbor, 920-839-9999
harborfishmarket-grille.com

Lure
10627 N Bay Shore Dr., Sister Bay, 920-854-8111
luredoorcounty.com

9

ENJOY A PILLOWY BITE OF HEAVEN
AT PRINCE OF PIEROGI

What the heck is a pierogi? Some call it a "delicious pillowy bite of heaven." Some say it's a ravioli stuffed with mashed potatoes. All agree it's a delicious gift from Polish culture. Throw in a "Dairy State" cheesy blend and pierogies will be your next favorite Door County meal.

Prince of Pierogi is Door County's premier Polish restaurant. Order at the window, grab a picnic table, and enjoy your pierogis alfresco or take them as carryout to enjoy at home. These dumplings are available with both traditional and contemporary fillings. Be comforted with cheese and potato or be daring with potato, cheddar, and jalapeño! Add a cabbage roll or some hunter's stew for the whole epicurean experience, then wash it all down with a Polish lager. Indulge your sweet tooth with a Door County cherry-and-cream-cheese pierogi or one stuffed with banana and Nutella.

9922 Water St. S, #6, Ephraim, 920-421-8619
princeofpierogi.com

10

DINE LAKESIDE

AT TOP DECK AND DONNY'S GLIDDEN LODGE

Perched right on the water, two restaurants on the east side of the peninsula capture classic Door County atmosphere and amazing Lake Michigan views.

The Top Deck at Gordon Lodge occupies a beautifully restored early-1900s boathouse with glossy wood interiors resembling a classic wooden boat. The dining room's extensive windows provide unobstructed views of North Bay and Lake Michigan. The menu has something for every dining intention, from small plates to handhelds and pasta to steak.

Donny's Glidden Lodge is part throwback Wisconsin supper club and part Old World resort serving traditional upscale cuisine, including steak and seafood. The cozy stone-and-wood building feels like an early 20th-century hunting lodge with a dark wood interior, stone fireplace, and vintage metal chandeliers. And while scoring a window seat is desirable, windows run the length of the restaurant, ensuring everyone has an outstanding view.

Top Deck Restaurant and Bar
1420 Pine Dr., Baileys Harbor, 920-839-2331
gordonlodge.com/top-deck-restaurant-bar

Donny's Glidden Lodge Restaurant
4670 Glidden Dr., Sturgeon Bay, 920-746-9460
donnysgliddenlodge.com

TIP

Even though you are on the Lake Michigan side of the peninsula, at Top Deck you can grab a glass of wine and enjoy a sunset. The shape of the bay and the Gordon Lodge property aims your sight lines toward the setting sun.

11

FIND YOUR SPIRITS
AT HATCH DISTILLING CO.

A hip, unique destination, Hatch Distilling Co. in Egg Harbor is a distillery specializing in spirits (vodka, bourbon, etc.) and other interesting liquors such as limoncello and apple brandy. Raising the hip-o-meter and delighting Ren-fair and fantasy gaming enthusiasts, Hatch also offers a unique collection of meads.

Hatch gets further props for sustainability. Dedicated to regional agriculture, it uses locally sourced grains and fruit. Also, the Hatch crew are beekeepers! Their bees are located around Door County on farms happy to share a little real estate. Hatch uses the honey to ferment its spirits and craft its meads.

The building is cool too, with a modern industrial vibe. A large, centrally located bar serves spirits and cocktails, or enjoy a flight on the patio. The neon "Mixed Meadia" sign points you to the cozy back bar serving meads and wines.

7740 WI-42, Egg Harbor, 920-543-3800
hatchdistilling.com

TIP

No food here. Just one-of-a-kind cocktails, spirits, and meads. And if you're adventurous or curious, spirits and meads can be sampled with flights.

ENJOY FIREPITS AND CONVIVIALITY
AT ONE BARREL BREWING

When kicking back with friends is on the itinerary, head to One Barrel Brewing in downtown Egg Harbor. You can't miss it! Firepits, loads of people, and cornhole games—conviviality abounds! If you're driving by, you'll think, "Wow! That's the place to be!" This popular brewery and taproom features pints of small-batch craft beers and wood-fired pizzas.

Honestly, no place captures the relaxed and fun atmosphere of Door County better than this welcoming taproom and beer garden. Bring the whole gang! Kids are welcome to have a blast, kid-style, while parents enjoy adult beverages. The beer garden is the main attraction with people and their canine pals enjoying themselves (and great beer!) around large firepits. The inside is also an inviting place to hang out for the afternoon and sample brews on tap, catch a game on TV, or enjoy a board game with the family.

4633 Market St., Egg Harbor, 920-868-5262
www.onebarrelbrewing.com

13

DRINK LIKE A LOCAL

Neighborhood bars are a Wisconsin staple. Rumor has it that Wisconsin has more bars than grocery stores. A variety of reasons are credited for this impressive accolade: One reason may be that Wisconsin was settled by immigrants from Germany and Switzerland—places famous for their drinking. One reason may be that plentiful waters led to a robust brewing industry. Some credit the Tavern League of Wisconsin, the largest association of beer sellers in the country. Whatever the reason, atmospheric corner bars abound in Wisconsin.

Door County features many cozy bars that convey strong Wisconsin feels. Northwoods-themed decorations (perhaps a canoe over the bar), cabin atmosphere, and Packers paraphernalia let you know that you've arrived. Then add a great selection of regional brews or a popular Wisconsin cocktail, give the beer something with which to be absorbed like a classic fish fry or Wisconsin brat, and your experience is complete.

SAMPLE SOME BREWS

Drinking like a local? Do a Door County pub crawl! Here are some classic Wisconsin bars on the peninsula:

Bayside Tavern

4160 Main St., Fish Creek, 920-868-3441
baysidetavern.com

Husby's

10641 N Bay Shore Dr., Sister Bay, 920-854-2624
husbysdoorcounty.com

Coyote Roadhouse

3026 County E, Baileys Harbor, 920-839-9192
coyote-roadhouse.com

The Baileys Harbor Cornerstone Pub

8123 WI-57, Baileys Harbor, 920-839-9001
baileysharborcornerstonepub.com

AC Tap

9322 WI-57, Baileys Harbor, 920-839-2426
On Facebook at AC Tap

Hitching Post Bar & Grill

4849 Glidden Dr., Sturgeon Bay, 920-818-1114
hitchingpostdoorcounty.com

Mink River Basin

12010 WI-42, Ellison Bay, 920-854-2250
theminkriverbasin.com

14

EAT ON THE ROOF
AT MEZZANINE

You're walking down the street thinking about where to have dinner when the enticing and aromatic food smells grab your attention. Then you notice the sound of people enjoying themselves over food and drink: a euphony of tinkling crystal, soft laughter, and background music. You look around and think, *Where is it coming from?* Then you look up! People are not only enjoying a sumptuous dinner, but they're doing so from a lofty outdoor setting with gentle lake breezes, festive lighting, and awesome views.

The Mezzanine is a hip rooftop restaurant in Egg Harbor, with minimalist furnishings, a large wood and corrugated-metal bar, and inviting festoon lighting. Mezzanine serves innovative twists on local favorites, and the rooftop seating offers outstanding views of the Egg Harbor Marina, harbor, and Green Bay beyond. Enjoy lunch with a view or dinner with a sunset.

7821 Horseshoe Bay Rd., Egg Harbor, 920-786-7698
mezzaninerooftop.com

MORE OUTDOOR DINING

Want more meals served alfresco from lofty perches with great views? Other favorite rooftop restaurants include:

Boathouse on the Bay

Boathouse on the Bay is a casual bar and grill with nautical themed decor and a west-facing, sunset-indulgent view over Sister Bay.

10716 N Bay Shore Dr., Sister Bay, 920-854-3223
boathousedcw.com

Chop Steakhouse

Chop Steakhouse is an upscale dinner-only restaurant featuring steak and seafood. In the heart of Sister Bay, Chop has west-facing, sunset-admiring rooftop seating and an elegant indoor dining room.

2345 Mill Rd., Sister Bay, 920-854-2700
chopdoorcounty.com

Loft

Loft features inviting second-story, open-air dining. No sunset views, but this restaurant commands an exciting location above the bustle of downtown Fish Creek. Loft has a casual grill menu for lunch and an elegant menu, with plenty of seafood options for the evening crowd.

4170 Main St., Fish Creek, 920-868-5242
loftfishcreek.com

15

SHOOT BITTERS
AT NELSEN'S HALL BITTERS PUB

When you find yourself on Washington Island and craving a shot of bitters, head to Nelsen's Hall Bitters Pub & Restaurant, serving lunch, dinner, and spirits (both in your shot glass and haunting the joint). Nelsen's is a historic tavern famous for serving shots of bitters with your burger (or infused in your burger!). That fame goes all the way back to Prohibition when Tom Nelsen, determined not to lose his bar to Prohibition laws, got a pharmacist's license and served bitters for medicinal purposes. He justified the speakeasy atmosphere of the hall as just a reflection of the civic purposes the hall provided the community.

Today, Nelsen's is considered the oldest continuously operating tavern in Wisconsin since the bitters "loophole" allowed it to survive Prohibition. The tavern's other claim to fame is being the largest purveyor of Angostura Bitters in the world, boasting over 10,000 shots annually.

1201 Main Rd., Washington Island, 920-847-2496
washingtonisland.com/nelsens-hall-bitters-pub-restaurant

16

INDULGE IN
ICE CREAM—YOU'RE ON VACATION!

You're on vacation, you've been biking and sightseeing and mini-putting and building sandcastles, it's getting warm outside, and . . . you're in the Dairy State! You know what that means . . . time for ice cream! (Or gelato or frozen custard or any number of frozen dairy delights available on the peninsula.)

Door County Ice Cream Factory serves premium homemade ice cream made on-site and in a wide variety of flavors. The historic shop has housed ice cream purveyors since the early 1900s.

Door County Creamery in the heart of Sister Bay features handcrafted gelato made from fresh goat milk in wonderfully decadent flavors. Other products include cheeses and soaps.

Not Licked Yet is known for creamy frozen yogurt and homemade pies. The colorful whimsical building, festive lighting, and lush garden draw you in. The shop sits on the banks of Fish Creek (the actual creek) and includes a kid-approved playground.

Door County Ice Cream Factory
11051 WI-42, Sister Bay, 920-854-9693
doorcountyicecream.com

Door County Creamery
10653 N Bay Shore Dr., Sister Bay, 920-854-3388
doorcountycreamery.com

Not Licked Yet
4054 Main St., Fish Creek, 920-868-2617
notlickedyet.com

DINE NOSTALGICALLY
AT A WISCONSIN SUPPER CLUB

Wisconsin is known for supper clubs. And while supper clubs have a rich history, the image of a Wisconsin-style supper club is colorfully rooted in the '50s and '60s. Friday night was always fish fry, Saturday night was always prime rib, your drink of choice was an old-fashioned, your table featured a relish tray, and the dance floor was hopping until the wee hours. Regional supper clubs were also celebrated for their blend of mid-century and Northwoods decor.

While we think about supper clubs with nostalgia, they are still a significant part of Wisconsin's restaurant culture. Whether it's your dining destination of choice or you want to check "Wisconsin Supper Club" off your bucket list, Door County's got you covered. The peninsula is dotted with popular supper clubs providing unique ambiance, satisfying menus, perfectly crafted cocktails, friendly faces, and a trusted going-out destination.

ENJOY A SUPPER CLUB

Check "Wisconsin Supper Club" off your bucket list with one of these Door County originals:

Alexander's of Door County

3667 WI-42, Fish Creek, 920-868-3532
alexandersofdoorcounty.com

Donny's Glidden Lodge Restaurant

4670 Glidden Dr., Sturgeon Bay, 920-746-9460
donnysgliddenlodge.com

The Mill Supper Club

4128 WI-42 WI-57, Sturgeon Bay, 920-743-5044
themillsupperclub.com

Nightingale Supper Club

1541 Egg Harbor Rd., Sturgeon Bay, 920-743-5593
nightingalesupperclub.com

Log Den

6626 WI-42, Egg Harbor, 920-868-3888
thelogden.com

18

FIND FOODIE INSPIRATION

Enthusiasts of all sorts find inspiration in Door County: nautical buffs, hikers and bikers, fishermen, theatergoers, kayakers and paddleboarders, art lovers, golfers, wine connoisseurs, birders, craft beer specialists, the list goes on and on. Gleefully, we can add enthusiastic diners to that list! All the restaurants on the peninsula are unique and independently owned, offering a plethora of dining options from satisfying bar fare to impressive high cuisine.

Whether you consider yourself a foodie, epicure, gourmand, or just hungry, you can make a Door County vacation out of restaurant hopping. The choice of unique restaurants across the peninsula can feel limitless. So loosen your belt and explore the Door, meal by meal.

Experience the hip, modern eatery, The Fashionable, in a historic downtown Ephraim building at 9996 Pioneer Lane (920-854-8008, thefashionabledc.com).

Enjoy unique, yet classic menu items in a modern and airy setting at Thyme Restaurant.

Thyme Restaurant
10339 WI-57, Sister Bay, 920-421-5113
thymedoorcounty.com

Fireside

Creative chef-inspired menu items with Cajun and creole themes in a cozy setting.

7755 WI-42, Egg Harbor, 920-868-4800
thefiresiderestaurant.com

Welcker's Lounge

Speakeasy-themed restaurant and lounge with a grand porch setting and elegant menu.

4192 Main St., Fish Creek, 920-868-5037
welckers.com

Waterfront

Upscale menu and dining experience with fabulous views.

10947 WI-42, Sister Bay, 920-854-5491
waterfront-dc.com

Inn at Cedar Crossing

Elegant dining in historic downtown.

336 Louisiana St., Sturgeon Bay, 920-743-4200
innatcedarcrossing.com

Crate Restaurant

Sushi, seafood, and steak in a hip, casual setting.

136 N 3rd Ave., Sturgeon Bay, 920-818-1333
craterestaurant.com

Sip

Fresh eatery, wine bar, and coffee shop with creative menu and colorful interior.

10326 N Water St., Ephraim, 920-857-5602
coffee@sipdoorcounty.com

19

SAMPLE WINES
ON THE DOOR COUNTY WINE TRAIL

Wine lovers, rejoice! Roll down the windows letting in the fresh lake breezes and hit the road for a day (or several) on the Door County Wine Trail. On the Wine Trail you can sample innovative wines from traditional local fruits or top-notch reds and whites from estate-harvested grapes. Also, you will enjoy the unique architecture and character of each winery and learn about its wine-making processes. Of course, the highlight is visiting the tasting rooms and sampling each winery's offerings.

The Door County Wine Trail website features a colorful map of the wineries' locations as well as information on the Door County Wine Passport, which offers a variety of discounts on everything from flights to purchases.

doorcountywinetrail.com

TIP

If everyone in your group wants to indulge in the sampling and no one wants to be the designated driver, check out Door County Trolley for tours featuring wine tasting at area wineries.

doorcountytrolley.com

A SAMPLING OF WINERIES ON THE TRAIL

Anchored Roots Vineyard & Winery
4873 Willow Rd., Egg Harbor, 920-868-4443
anchoredrootswine.com

Simon Creek Vineyard & Winery

5896 Bochek Rd., Sturgeon Bay, 920-746-9307
simoncreekvineyard.com

Door 44 Winery

5464 County P, Sturgeon Bay, 920-388-4400
44wineries.com

Door Peninsula Winery

5806 WI-42, Carlsville, 800-551-5049
dcwine.com

Harbor Ridge Winery

4690 Rainbow Ridge Ct., Egg Harbor, 920-868-4321
harborridgewinery.com

Lake Fire Winery

8054 WI-57, Baileys Harbor, 920-839-9992
lakefirewinery.com

Red Oak Winery

5781 WI-42, Sturgeon Bay, 920-743-7729
redoakwinery.com

20

DINE ELEGANTLY
IN A HISTORIC SETTING

While exquisite cuisine is the draw, add an interesting historic building, and you have a unique Door County dining experience.

Chives in Baileys Harbor is an elegant restaurant featuring innovative gourmet cuisine. Located in a historic building, the decor is cozy and intimate with bay windows providing Lake Michigan views. Chives also hosts food trucks at its lake-facing courtyard for a casual yet foodie meal.

Burton's on the Bay at Alpine Resort features upscale cuisine in a newly renovated restaurant with mid-century and Great Camp vibes. Burton's also has lovely patio seating with great Green Bay views. Enjoy a sunset with your cocktail.

Barringers in Fish Creek features steak and seafood in a historic building dating back to 1910. The unique building has a loft area and patio seating. The dining room has an old New England feel with white ceiling beams and a big stone fireplace.

Chives Door County
8041 WI-57, Baileys Harbor, 920-839-2000
chivesdoorcounty.com

Burton's on the Bay
7715 Alpine Rd., Egg Harbor, 920-868-3000
alpineresort.com/dine/burtons-on-the-bay

Barringers Restaurant
1 Spruce St., Fish Creek, 920-868-5445
barringersdoorcounty.com

DRINK UNIQUELY
AT SWAY

Because drinking good beer and eating good food should be fun, relaxed, and social, along came Sway, a taproom (and bakery?!) in Baileys Harbor. Describing their beers as "balanced and easy drinking," Sway is a craft-brew taproom. Housed in the former Door County Brewing facility, the cozy taproom located above the fermentation cellar includes relaxed indoor seating and a hopping (no pun intended) outdoor patio.

The beers are uniquely aged and fermented for offerings such as County Yarrow, an oak-fermented saison with foraged yarrow, or Where the Light Turns Night, a foeder-fermented amber lager. But here's the kicker: Sway also has an on-site bakery with breakfast and dessert pastries, coffee and tea, and a kitchen serving up unique sandwiches and dips throughout the day.

2434 County F, Baileys Harbor, 920-241-3562
swaybeer.com

EAT PIZZA WILDLY
AT WILD TOMATO

To many, pizza is the perfect food. At Wild Tomato, it's true! The pizzas at this popular and often acclaimed restaurant are wood fired to perfection with outstanding ingredients and creative combinations and are complemented by other good stuff on the menu.

But the delicious 'za is only part of the wow! While you're stuffing yourself with pizza, you're contributing to the Door County community. Wild Tomato has great missions (beyond the goal of making great pizza). They are dedicated to sustainably sourcing their fresh ingredients from local suppliers, and they provide charitable support to local organizations. The menu features a monthly Donation Creation: a pie for which the sales benefit a local nonprofit.

The restaurants, located in Sister Bay and Fish Creek are fun too! Airy and modern with great outdoor seating and prime locations. Also, the Sister Bay restaurant has easy access to the beach.

Wild Tomato Sister Bay
10677 N Bay Shore Dr., Sister Bay, 920-854-4685

Wild Tomato Fish Creek
4023 WI-42, Fish Creek, 920-868-3095

wildtomatopizza.com

BE ITALIAN!

If the verdant fields, vineyards, and wineries have you craving pasta, three authentic Italian restaurants deliver classic Mediterranean village vibes and will have you exclaiming, "Il cibo è fantastico!"

Osteri Tre Tassi boasts authentic Mediterranean cuisine with fresh farm-to-table ingredients. The restaurant is in a historic inn built in the early 1900s. The cozy atmosphere blends old New England with rustic Italian and the grounds evoke an Italian country-village feel. Enjoy homemade pasta and Italian wines.

Villagios Italian Steakhouse offers traditional steak, seafood, and pasta selections with a modern twist in an earthy restaurant with a warm yet modern interior. The restaurant elicits the joy of a celebratory Italian feast.

Della Porta features southern Italian fare and Napoli pizzas made from seasonal ingredients sourced from local farms. The restaurant, part of the Blue Bear, has an inviting patio.

Osteria Tre Tassi
11976 Mink River Rd., Ellison Bay, 920-309-8390
tretassi.com

Villagios Italian Steakhouse
4655 County E, Egg Harbor, 920-890-2190
mojorestaurantgroup.com/villaggios

Della Porta Trattoria e Pizzeria Napoletana
12029 WI-42, Ellison Bay, 920-633-4014
dellaportadc.com

Live performances lakeside
at Peninsula Players Theater

MUSIC
AND ENTERTAINMENT

24

FIND MUSIC, LAUGHS, AND FOLKLORE
AT NORTHERN SKY THEATER

Deep in Peninsula State Park, you might hear the wild sounds of . . . laughter and singing? Northern Sky Theater has been delighting audiences from this open-air amphitheater since the 1970s with original, folklore-based productions loaded with comedy and music. The shows celebrate (and often lovingly poke fun at) the heritage and culture of Door County, northern Wisconsin, and the Midwest in general with stories that are often as poignant as they are funny.

In 2019, Northern Sky opened a new facility, the Northern Sky Theater's Creative Center and Gould Theater, which features year-round productions and serves as the organization's headquarters. While an indoor theater, it maintains the woodsy, outdoor feel of the park amphitheater. The walls of the auditorium are clad in reclaimed barn wood from across the peninsula and feature floor-to-ceiling doors that open to allow natural light and lovely views.

Northern Sky Theater
9058 County Rd. A, Fish Creek, 920-854-6117
northernskytheater.com

Peninsula State Park Amphitheater
9462 Shore Rd., Fish Creek, 920-868-3258
dnr.wisconsin.gov/topic/parks/peninsula/recreation/theater

ENJOY LIVE MUSIC ALFRESCO
WITH PEG EGAN PAC

Live music under the stars is a lovely way to spend a summer evening. One of the most popular places for music alfresco is the Peg Egan concert series held in the Egg Harbor Amphitheater with acclaimed international musicians performing a variety of musical genres on a modern open-air stage. An expansive grassy lawn provides the audience seating, with concertgoers feasting on artful picnics, celebrating with friends and fine wines, and enjoying world-class music, lake breezes, and the beautiful backdrop of Egg Harbor. The concerts have a big-city feel with quaint village charm, and the performances are free.

So be part of the scene and enjoy a concert under an early evening Door County sky. Pack an elegant picnic and your favorite bottle of wine, or secure a spot ahead of time, drop off your chairs, and head into town to grab dinner at your favorite Egg Harbor eatery before the show.

7840 Church St., Egg Harbor, 920-493-5979
facebook.com/PegEganPAC

26

CLIMB ABOARD
A SISTER BAY SCENIC BOAT TOUR

We all love gazing out at Lake Michigan and Green Bay, but for an opportunity to view the spectacular shoreline from the water, climb aboard a fun and informational Sister Bay Scenic Boat Tour. One tour offers views of the ledges and caves of Peninsula State Park as well as the Eagle Point Lighthouse. Or choose the ride that cruises along Sister Bay's north shore, past Ellison Bay's majestic bluffs to Gills Rock and the Death's Door Crossing.

On both tours you will be blown away by the size of the cliffs created by the Niagara Escarpment (aren't we in the flat Midwest?) and impressed by the houses perched upon them. The knowledgeable and entertaining tour narrators regale you with history and lore. Boats are double-decker offering shade or sun and feature a bar for drinks and snacks.

Fish Creek Scenic Boat Tours also feature cruises along the rugged Peninsula State Park shoreline and a route along Door County's fabled "Millionaire's Row."

Door County Boats
Sister Bay Scenic Boat Tours
10707 N Bay Shore Dr., Sister Bay, 920-421-4444
doorcountyboats.com

Fish Creek Scenic Boat Tours
9448 Spruce Street, Fish Creek, 920-421-4442
doorcountybywater.com/fishcreekscenicboattours

TIP

Want to navigate your own excursion? Door County Boats rents pontoons, speedboats, and Jet Skis from two locations: Sister Bay and Egg Harbor.

Also, while we featured specific tours and Door County Boats rentals, the peninsula is home to many other quality boat-tour companies and boat-rental companies. If you want to launch from a different village or need different accommodations, a quick online search or a stroll through one of the village's marinas will help you find the tour or boat rental that is right for you.

27

CATCH A CONCERT IN AN ECCENTRIC VENUE
AT FISHSTOCK

The ’60s had Woodstock . . . Door County has Fishstock! First timers will be delightfully surprised by this impressive yet unassuming music venue. The Fishstock Concert Series has been providing top-notch live music to Door County audiences for over two decades. Performances are primarily folk music, but a variety of genres by national and regional artists are included in the concert schedule.

While the quality of the artists promises an evening of outstanding music, the sound is enhanced by the venue itself, a 100-year-old barn with impressive acoustics and a professional sound system. The barn is open at one end, and the rustic walls have gaps between the boards, allowing a breezy open-air ambiance. Reserved indoor seating and adjacent outdoor seating is ample and can accommodate a large audience.

3127 County F, Fish Creek, 414-659-1521
fishstockmusic.com

TIP

Picnicking is encouraged before or during the show on the grounds around the barn, but it’s all BYO. No food or beverages are available for sale.

28

LEAVE THE DRIVING
TO DOOR COUNTY TROLLEY

Wouldn't it be nice to have a designated driver just so you can watch the scenery instead of the road? Let Door County Trolley do the driving for you! A ride on one of these cute red trolleys is a popular Door County attraction and a great way to get the lay of the land. From a seat on the trolley, you can sightsee without needing to access your GPS or to stop abruptly to take a picture.

For a picturesque overview of Door County, try the Narrated Scenic Tour focusing on the Green Bay side of the peninsula or the Lakeside Scenic Tour for a ride on the Lake Michigan side. Both tours not only deliver magnificent views but also provide entertaining Door County information, history, and lore.

8030 WI-42, Egg Harbor, 920-868-1100
doorcountytrolley.com

TIP

To add some spooky to your adventure, explore the dark side of Door County with the Ghost Tour of Door County aboard the Trolley of the Doomed, the Murder & Mayhem Tour, or the Haunted Pub Crawl. Or, on a less ghostly note, leave the driving to Door County Trolley and embark on one of their many wine tours or pub crawls.

MAKE ART
AT HANDS ON

Everywhere you go in Door County, you can see art, buy art, or play next to art. Are you feeling inspired? Are your kids' inner Picassos showing? Well, it's time to turn "I could do that" into "Look what I did!" Get your own hands dirty, get your creative juices flowing, and leave for home with the best souvenir ever: a piece of art created by you.

Hands On Art Studio is possibly the most colorful place on the peninsula. With a laid-back and fun vibe, the beautiful and artsy grounds include the Art Barn with ceramics and mosaics, a glass studio for fused-glass projects, a painting studio, and the Workshop, which houses board sign and metal art painting and stamped jewelry making. Just stop in (no reservation needed) to indulge your artistic whim or go all in with a class in wheel throwing or metalworking.

3655 Peninsula Players Rd., Fish Creek, 920-868-9311
handsonartstudio.com

TIP

The ceramics studio is very popular for entertaining kids, especially on rainy days! However, if you're traveling kid-free, don't let that scare you. You can enjoy a relaxed, focused, artsy time in the other studios.

BE SURPRISED
BY THE CHERRY HUT

The Cherry Hut might capture your attention as another wonderful Door County farm market. After all, the exterior captures the vibe of its former life as a 1950s roadside attraction selling canned goods and postcards. But you're in for a surprise as the Cherry Hut is a fun and unique Door County destination. It's still a farm market with locally sourced canned goods as well as a wide variety of gourmet foods. It's also a gift shop with souvenirs, kitchen wares, and fun stuff.

However, to give it "destination" cred, the Cherry Hut features retro decor as an homage to its past. It's a taproom for Sturgeon Bay's Bridge Up Brewing. It's a restaurant with gourmet hot dogs, unique tacos, and rib tips in outrageous flavors. And, putting a bow on this eclectic and wonderful package, it's a live-music venue on weekends during the summer.

The Cherry Hut
Bridge Up North Taproom
8813 WI-42, Fish Creek, 920-868-4450
doorcountycherryhut.com
bridgeupbrewing.com

HEAR LIVE MUSIC EVERY NIGHT!

CONCERTS IN THE PARK SERIES

What's better than hanging out in the park listening to live music on summer evenings? How about a concert in a park every night of the week?! Door County is made up of a number of quaint villages, and to the joy of live-music lovers, the villages collaborate for the Summertime Concerts in the Park series. Five different villages host live music on a specific weeknight during the summer. Performances cover a variety of genres, and each village boasts a unique, public, open-air music facility. Each venue is near local restaurants for a pre-show bite to eat. If you're at the Egg Harbor, Fish Creek, or Sister Bay concert, make sure the sunset is part of the itinerary. So, grab some chairs, snacks, and maybe a little bug spray, and head to the town park for a summer full of music.

Check out the websites for Baileys Harbor, Ephraim, Fish Creek, Sister Bay, Egg Harbor, and Sturgeon Bay for their concert schedules.

baileysharbor.com/events
ephraim-doorcounty.com/events
visitfishcreek.com/events
sisterbay.com/events/p/sisterbayconcerts
eggharbordoorcounty.org/events/concerts-in-the-park
sturgeonbay.net/special-events/harmony-by-the-bay-concert-series

CATCH NOSTALGIA AND A MOVIE
AT SKYWAY DRIVE-IN

For a truly nostalgic experience and a fun way to entertain the kiddies, catch a flick under the stars at Skyway Drive-In Theatre! With only about 300 drive-in theaters in operation across the US, Skyway is truly a Door County gem.

This theater, lovingly maintained by a new generation of family owners, runs current and family-friendly movies. The modernized sound system can run through your car's audio. You can bring a portable radio if you prefer to sit outside your car, and if you want the true vintage experience, old-timey speakers are available in a couple of rows. The snack bar offers pizza, hot dogs, nachos, candy, ice cream, and a variety of beverages.

So, pack up the kids, the blankets, the lawn chairs, and even the dog (as long as he's on a leash), and head out to the Skyway for a throwback fun, family night out.

3475 WI-42, Fish Creek, 920-854-9938
doorcountydrivein.com

HIT THE HIGH NOTES
AT BIRCH CREEK

What's more exciting than a screaming trumpet hitting the high notes in a big band jazz performance or the vibrant, rhythmic music of a steel drum band? How about a world-class residential music program set against a beautiful Door County backdrop. Birch Creek Music Performance Center is a summer music academy for aspiring students offering retreats led by acclaimed professional musicians from around the globe in the genres of big band jazz, symphony, and percussion/steel pan/world music. Adults can indulge their musical aspirations as well with summer retreats for adult learners.

The public gloriously benefits from the Birch Creek program as concerts are held throughout the summer with performances by students as well as the faculty's professional musicians. Performances are held in the Dutton Concert Barn on the Birch Creek Campus or in an open-air gazebo on the grounds, as well as other venues around the peninsula.

3821 County E, Egg Harbor, 920-868-3763
birchcreek.org

DISCOVER WORLD-CLASS ENTERTAINMENT AT DOOR COMMUNITY AUDITORIUM

Most entertainment venues in Door County are pretty relaxed (and outdoors). If you're in the mood for a refined experience in a sophisticated theater, perhaps a high-caliber symphony performance or famous musician, look no further than Door Community Auditorium (DCA). Considered the peninsula's premier performing arts center, the DCA's annual program includes a wide variety of cultural performances including nationally known artists, touring acts, world music, and dance.

DCA is also the primary site of the Peninsula Music Festival, a world-class symphonic music series held every August. According to the festival's website, "The DCA was built specifically for the Festival Orchestra and is ideal for symphonic music."

The majority of programs are held in the summer months. However, the DCA is open year-round with holiday programs and lectures in winter months. The theater also serves as a venue for music and theater productions by local schools.

Door Community Auditorium
3926 WI-42, Fish Creek, 920-868-2728
dcauditorium.org

Peninsula Music Festival
musicfestival.com

35

TAKE A SUNSET LIVE MUSIC CRUISE

Up and down the west coast of the peninsula (and where the view allows on the east coast), people seek out spots to take in the magnificent Door County sunsets. For a front-row seat to the majestic show, climb aboard a Sunset Live Music Cruise.

Nightly cruises are available from both Fish Creek and Sister Bay harbors. The routes vary depending on the time of the sunset and offer unobstructed views of the colorful western sky and the sinking sun's reflection on the waters of Green Bay. The cruises provide spectacular panoramas of the rugged Peninsula State Park coastline as the light, color, and shadow dance across the dramatic canvas of cliffs and caves. Live music provides a unique ambiance to the experience. You are invited to bring your own beverages for a chill, memorable, and totally Door County experience.

Sister Bay Scenic Boat Tours
10707 N Bay Shore Dr., Sister Bay, 920-421-4444
doorcountyboats.com

Fish Creek Scenic Boat Tours
9448 Spruce St., Fish Creek, 920-421-4442
doorcountybywater.com

GO PLUM LOCO
FOR ANIMALS

It's wonderful when a vacation not only dishes up big fun with wholesome nature-based activities, but also provides lessons in being a good human. To encourage the good human in your kids, put Plum Loco Animal Farm on your itinerary.

Plum Loco is a family-owned farm animal sanctuary that shares its gentle beasts with the public. It has a mission firmly rooted in giving animals safe and happy lives filled with love and dignity. Your kids will go "plum loco" with all the furry cuteness on display including ponies, goats, sheep, miniature pigs, and more!

In addition to opportunities to pet and feed (and pet and pet and pet) a variety of gentle animals, the Plum Loco grounds include its Play-Farm Village with a variety of kiddo-sized buildings to play in and pint-sized tractors to ride. The whole experience inspires big imaginations and even bigger hearts.

4431 Plum Bottom Rd., Egg Harbor, 920-743-1617
plumlocoanimalfarm.com

TIP

Plum Loco is a fun family fall destination (weekends only) with pumpkin painting for the kids and festive fall decoration around the farm.

HAVE A TOE-TAPPIN' GOOD TIME

AT THE FIDDLER'S FARM

For a toe-tappin' good time, catch a show at the Fiddler's Farm just south of Sturgeon Bay. The Fiddler's Farm features regional and national artists performing primarily country, Western swing, and bluegrass concerts in a beautiful and family-friendly setting. As its website states, Fiddler's Farm brings a little Branson to Southern Door County.

The shows are performed in an airy historic barn that also serves as a wedding venue. The barn has ample seating with good sight lines and great sound. The audience size is big enough to generate energy, but small enough for performances to feel intimate. Glittery chandeliers (remember, it's also a wedding venue) and festoon lighting add to the festive atmosphere. Grab a preshow bite at the Burger Shack or snazzy gift at The Coop.

Watch The Fiddler's Farm Facebook page for up-to-date happenings, concerts, and off-season events.

6951 County Rd. C, Sturgeon Bay, 920-559-3460
thefiddlersfarm.com
facebook.com/thefiddlersfarm

TREAT YOUR GUITAR TO VACATION AT THE HOLIDAY MUSIC MOTEL

Here's a cool combo: Stay in retro style while supporting a hip local music scene! The Holiday Music Motel in Sturgeon Bay is a mid-century gem with vintage decor and an iconic neon sign. Over time, the motel has been involved in music recording and production and is the inspiration for Holiday Music Motel the band, with over 200 members who have been involved in the local music scene.

If you're staying at the motel and want to catch some local entertainment, head next door to the Tambourine Lounge, an arts collaborative that hosts not only live music but unique writers' open-mic nights. The motel and Tambourine Lounge are affiliated with the Steel Bridge Creative Foundation, an organization dedicated to the preservation of Sturgeon Bay's historic steel bridge, historic downtown, and local music and arts.

Holiday Music Motel
30 N 1st Ave., Sturgeon Bay, 920-743-5571
holidaymusicmotel.com

The Tambourine Lounge
59 N 2nd Ave., Sturgeon Bay, 920-743-5571
facebook.com/tambourineLounge

Steel Bridge Creative Foundation
steelbridgecreativefoundation.org

EXPERIENCE ISLAND MAGIC

AT TRUEBLOOD PERFORMING ARTS CENTER

Washington Island may seem remote; after all, it takes a ferry ride to get there. But this dynamic community holds its own in terms of entertainment thanks to the Trueblood Performing Arts Center (TPAC), a multipurpose theater that holds over 250 people and provides a community performance venue. The cool modern building has a commanding presence, an industrial feel, and gives a nod to Door County's nautical roots with exterior fabric sails. The site includes an expansive lawn for outside performances "On the Green."

The diverse TPAC schedule includes music performances of all genres, storytelling, plays, community events, fundraisers, comedy, you name it! TPAC is also the home of Washington Island Radio, an FM radio station dedicated to promoting music, information, history, and community with a goal (as noted on their website) of sending "some island magic out on the airwaves."

Trueblood Performing Arts Center
870 Main Rd., Washington Island, 920-847-2528
tpacwashingtonisland.com

Washington Island Radio
washingtonislandradio.com

40

ENJOY CHAMBER ENSEMBLES WITH MIDSUMMER'S MUSIC

Classical music lovers, rejoice! While live music can be found everywhere across the peninsula, Midsummer's Music delivers world-class chamber music to Door County's performing-arts community. A rich variety of classical arrangements is delivered by varying ensembles from Midsummer's 20-plus distinguished musicians who hail from around the country. Affiliated with Midsummer is the Griffon String Quartet, a professional ensemble performing as part of the Midsummer lineup as well as providing community performances and programs throughout northeastern Wisconsin off season.

Midsummer's performances are enhanced by unique settings, varying acoustics, and the intimacy of the events. Concerts are held in a variety of venues around the peninsula, including galleries, churches, music pavilions, and performance halls. The intimate settings allow the audience to experience and enjoy not only outstanding music, but the personality of the performers and synergy of the ensemble.

Midsummer's Music, Ltd.
920-854-7088
midsummersmusic.com

Griffon String Quartet
midsummersmusic.com/the-griffon-string-quartet

41

END THE DAY
WITH A SPECTACULAR SUNSET

Despite all of the entertainment offered across the peninsula, the main event most nights is the sunset. After a day filled with fun activities and the great outdoors, Mother Nature gives you one last hurrah as the sun disappears in the western skies, turning them glorious hues of gold, pink, orange, purple and red, and reflecting this magnificent display on the watery surfaces of lakes and bays. So grab a western-facing view, in town or out, up on a rocky ledge or down at beach level, on a picnic blanket or an alfresco barstool, and enjoy the best show in Door County.

If you're on the east side of the peninsula, a couple of locations well-positioned by the geometry of a bay or pier will deliver a sunset. Also, watching the sunrise over Lake Michigan is a popular event in Baileys Harbor and Jacksonport.

SUPERB SUNSET SPOTS

Sunset spots around Door County are plentiful but here are some recommendations:

For easy access to dinner before or after Mother Nature's show, head to the heart of Sister Bay or Egg Harbor.

Sister Bay Beach or Harbor
2362 Mill Rd., Sister Bay

Harbor View Park
7809 WI-42, Egg Harbor

For a uniquely Door County sunset, a spot on Anderson Dock in Ephraim lets you not only watch the sun set over the Bay, but the sunsets' colors as they wash over the charming white buildings of Ephraim.

Anderson Dock
3083 Anderson Ln., Ephraim

For a bluff setting high above the water, bring a blanket to relax and enjoy the view from Ellison Bluff County Park or grab a spot at one of the many overlooks in Peninsula State Park.

Ellison Bluff County Park
12050 Ellison Bluff Rd., Ellison Bay

Peninsula State Park
9462 Shore Rd., Fish Creek

On the east side of the peninsula, grab a glass of wine at the Top Deck and head out to the end of the pier at Gordon Lodge.

The Top Deck at Gordon Lodge
1420 Pine Dr., Baileys Harbor

Explore Cave Point County Park by kayak

SPORTS AND RECREATION

KAYAK
A RUGGED SHORELINE

With so much water in Door County, from Lake Michigan to tranquil bays, and an impressive array of shorelines, from beaches to rocky towering bluffs, kayaking adventures are abundant.

To explore the famous shoreline and caves at Cave Point County Park, start at Schauer Park and head south. If the lake is calm, brave souls can paddle into the caves! Continue toward Whitefish Dunes State Park and pull up onto the soft sand for a relaxing break before heading back.

For a view of the towering cliffs of Peninsula State Park, put in at Ephraim pier or beach and paddle the south side of Eagle Harbor. On the return trip, take in spectacular views of picturesque Ephraim with its white clapboard buildings ascending the hillside.

Schauer Park
Schauer Rd., east of Cave Point Dr., Sturgeon Bay
jacksonport.net/area-parks

Cave Point County Park
5360 Schauer Rd., Sturgeon Bay, 920-746-9959
co.door.wi.gov/554/Cave-Point-County-Park

Peninsula State Park
9462 Shore Rd., Fish Creek, 920-868-3258
dnr.wisconsin.gov/topic/parks/peninsula

Ephraim Pier/Beach/Waterfront
WI-42, Ephraim, 54211

TIP

For a more serene and less crowded paddling experience, head to the Mink River Estuary. Put in at the public boat landing in Rowleys Bay. Head north hugging the shore or out across the open water toward the estuary's mouth. Quietly paddle into the calm and reed-lined waterways while you listen for the songs of the numerous birds. Go as deep into the estuary as desired before turning around and heading out.

If you don't want to go it alone, kayak tours are available!

Door County Kayak Tours
doorcountykayaktours.com

Peninsula Kayak Company
peninsulakayakcompany.com

Lakeshore Adventures Kayak Tours
doorcountykayaking.com/door-county-kayak-tour-info

43

HIT THE BEACH!

With hundreds of miles of shoreline, hitting the beach is big fun in Door County, and the peninsula delivers a truly beachy vibe. The reasons for loving the beach are as unique as the people who love it, and for every individual, sand-filled aspiration, Door County delivers a beach.

Door County features many in-town beaches, where your beach day can include a short walk to an ice cream cone, lunch, or your next beer. Popular sandy and shallow beaches are great for spending a day with the kids in gentle waves and on soft sands. The peninsula also has remote beaches for a quiet, reflective, Zen beach experience.

With more than 24 beaches, you will find the perfect beach for your vacation. So grab your flip-flops, beach towel, sandcastle tools, and sunscreen, and hit the beach!

BEACHES EVERYWHERE!

"In the middle of it all" beaches:

Waterfront Park/Sister Bay Beach
Otumba Beach, Sturgeon Bay
Ephraim Public Beach
Amclam Beach, Baileys Harbor
Fish Creek Public Beach

Sandy, family-fun beaches:

Egg Harbor Beach
Baileys Harbor/Ridges Town Park Beach
Nicolet Beach, Peninsula State Park
Lakeside Park Beach, Jacksonport
Ellison Bay Community Park Beach
Sand Bay Town Park Beach, Liberty Grove

Secluded and beautiful beaches:

Whitefish Dunes State Park
Rock Island Beach
Pebble Beach, Sister Bay
Schoolhouse Beach, Washington Island
Percy Johnson Memorial County Park Beach, Washington Island
Sand Dunes Park Beach, Washington Island
Newport Beach, Newport State Park

TAKE A HIKE!

Whether you're planning a hiking vacation or simply a morning walk, Door County is your dream destination. The peninsula offers a myriad of options for hikers and walkers of all abilities set against a wide range of stunning backgrounds. With five state parks, more than 15 county parks, and many land trusts and nature preserves, trail options are abundant. Hikers can find well-marked trails with a variety of terrains, distances, and views. Explore paths through birches, evergreens, and maples or explore rocky coastlines and stunning water views. And if you just want to go for a walk, every road across the peninsula features abundant natural beauty.

For a hike that has it all, check out the Fern and Lynd Point Trail in Newport State Park. While not long, these trails traverse many of the natural features Door County is known for such as rocky shorelines, marshy inlands, and wooded areas. The trails are well marked and maintained.

475 WI-42, Ellison Bay, 920-854-2500
dnr.wisconsin.gov/topic/parks/newport

TIP

For a multiday adventure, hop on part of a longer trail. In Door County you can access the Ahnapee State Trail or the 1,200-mile Ice Age Trail.

BE MIND BLOWN

BY A DARK SKY

If you haven't been gobsmacked by all the natural beauty of Door County by day, just wait until the sun goes down. Newport State Park in Ellison Bay is not only considered Wisconsin's only wilderness state park but is also the first state park in Wisconsin to be designated an International Dark Sky Park! This is some serious cred, as there are fewer than 20 parks in the US and fewer than 50 parks on the whole planet with that designation.

As a Dark Sky Park, Newport delivers a mind-blowing, breathtaking view of the massive universe we humbly inhabit. For some serious stargazing and constellation spotting, head to the beach or stake out one of the recommended viewing areas. Cozy up on a blanket and let the awesome celestial display surround you, or bust out your telescope and enjoy the spectacle of the glorious night sky.

475 WI-42, Ellison Bay, 920-854-2500
dnr.wisconsin.gov/topic/parks/newport/darksky

46

AWE AND TERROR—
EXPLORE A SHIPWRECK

Shipwrecks inspire within us both awe and terror. Maybe it's the realization of the power and fury of the Great Lakes. Maybe it's that deep in the dark waters, a piece of history is preserved. Whatever the draw, whatever the awe, exploring shipwrecks is a unique Door County activity.

The waters surrounding the peninsula are home to the remains of more than 200 shipwrecks, with some of them explorable. To combine shipwrecks and recreation, consider a shipwreck boat or raft tour. Or better yet, get a close-up view by kayak! Shipwreck kayak tours are offered for Lake Michigan sites off Baileys Harbor and for sites in the waters near Death's Door off Door Bluff Headlands County Park. (Don't worry, it's not as scary as it sounds.)

Shoreline Boat Tours
120 N Madison Ave., Sturgeon Bay
8132 WI-57, Baileys Harbor, 920-854-4707
shorelinedoorcounty.com/baileys-harbor-cruise

Lakeshore Adventures Kayak Tours
8113 WI-57, Baileys Harbor, 920-839-2055
doorcountykayaking.com/door-county-kayak-tour-info/clear-bottom-shipwreck-tour

Door County Adventure Rafting
3899 WI-42, Fish Creek, 920-559-6106
doorcountyadventurerafting.com
doorcountyboattours.com

IMMERSE IN
SCENERY BY BIKE

There's no better way to immerse yourself in Door County's impressive scenery than on a bike! For a "best of" ride, saddle up in Murphy County Park, south of Egg Harbor. Map your ride to follow these roads along the lakefront north to Fish Creek: Horseshoe Bay, White Cliff, Juddville (a climb!), Highway 42 (briefly), Peninsula Players, Gibraltar Bluff, and Cottage Row.

This fun route takes you past farms, fields, bluffs, woods, and the classic Alpine Resort (don't miss the bluff view at the stop sign!) before entering Egg Harbor. From there, enjoy a speedy downhill coast and meandering ride on shady, tree-lined roads with views of lake houses and soaring cliffs. The grand finale: Cottage Row Road takes you down its famous switchback then along its storied and elegant residences, delivering you into quaint Fish Creek for a well-deserved break at one of its many cafés.

7119 Bay Shore Dr., Egg Harbor, 920-746-9959
co.door.wi.gov/542/Frank-E-Murphy-County-Park

TIP

With rustic roads, county highways, and trails, Door County has a ride for every skill level, desired difficulty, and tire size!

SADDLE UP
AT KURTZ CORRAL

Skilled horsemen and first-time buckaroos alike will love sauntering through the Door County countryside on the back of a majestic beast. Connect with nature, admire the beautiful scenery, and enjoy the relaxing ride with the rhythmic motion of your horse's gait.

Kurtz Corral, just south of Jacksonport, is the go-to destination for horseback riding on the peninsula. With hundreds of acres of natural settings, the riding trails meander through wooded areas and pastures. Safety is a priority for both guests and horses, so be prepared to take part in an instructional session and follow all protocol. For little cowboys and cowgirls under age 6, Kurtz delivers with a 30-minute arena ride. Be ready on your ride home from your Door County vacation to answer the call of, "Dad, can we get a pony?"

Kurtz is open year-round! Consider booking a trail ride when Mother Nature is flaunting her autumn brilliance or wintry snow-covered landscape.

5712 Howard Ln., Sturgeon Bay, 920-743-6742
kurtzcorral.com

49

FIND YOUR BALANCE
ON A STAND-UP PADDLEBOARD

Whether you're after a little zen or just a fun way to splash around with your friends, make sure your itinerary includes stand-up paddleboarding. Door County offers as many unique places to SUP as reasons people enjoy the sport. Here are a few favorites:

For easy access to board rental for a couple of hours paddling with friends, try the Sister Bay Beach, Egg Harbor Beach, or Nicolet Beach in Peninsula State Park.

To paddle next to impressive cliffs, put your board in at Garrett Bay just north of Ellison Bay, and if your balance allows, look up and enjoy the majestic views of the Door Bluff Headlands.

If you're after action, head to Baileys Harbor, one of the largest bays in Door County, and put your skills to the test in Lake Michigan waves.

For the zen factor, check out the calm waters and unique environmental vibe of Mink River Estuary in Rowleys Bay, a quiet off-the-beaten-path destination.

Garrett Bay Road Boat Ramp
1310 Garrett Bay Rd., Ellison Bay, 920-854-5448
doorcountynorth.org/garrett-bay-park

Mink River Preserve
11590 Mink River Rd., Ellison Bay, 608-266-0394
nature.org/en-us/get-involved/how-to-help/
places-we-protect/mink-river-estuary

50

CATCH A FERRY
TO WASHINGTON ISLAND

The end of the road at the top of the peninsula is just the beginning of a grand adventure! Catch a ferry for a scenic ride across Death's Door to Washington Island. The kiddos will love the novelty of driving your car onto a boat, or you can leave the car at Northport Pier and bike aboard. The ferries have upper-level, open-air seating for great views as you pass Plum, Detroit, and Pilot Islands.

If you want to explore all of Washington Island or if you're lodging there, you will probably want your car. However, the island is very bike-friendly and bike and moped rentals are available. The island is famous for its beaches and features other visitor attractions. But if it's all about the ferry ride, head to the north end of the island, and you can grab another ferry to Rock Island.

Washington Island Ferry Line
Northport Pier, 215 WI-42, Ellison Bay, 920-847-2546
wisferry.com

Check out the Washington Island website for
all of the cool stuff to do there:
washingtonisland.com

TIP

Rock Island is beautiful but remote. The Rock Island Boathouse (also called the Thodarson Boathouse), on the National Register of Historic Places, is architecturally significant, has an interesting history, and is available to tour. Otherwise, Rock Island is all about hiking and camping and could be a challenging destination for those who have difficulty walking.

dnr.wisconsin.gov/topic/parks/rockisland

51

GOLF WITH A VIEW

The sweet ecstasy (or agony) of teeing up your ball, feeling the lake breeze in your hair, and eyeing the lush fairway in anticipation of the satisfying "whack" of a well-placed drive. If you'd always rather be golfing, Door County's got you covered.

Alpine Resort is an iconic (and challenging) 18-hole course nestled along the shores of Green Bay. With hills, bluffs, and woods, Alpine offers a variety of picturesque and challenging fairways. Alpine's blue ninth hole, the "Bluff Hole," offers a panoramic view and has been called "the most scenic hole in the State of Wisconsin."

Peninsula State Park Golf Course may beg to differ on that "most scenic" hole title, boasting awe-inspiring views of the Village of Ephraim and Eagle Harbor from atop lofty ledges. This legendary course, over 100 years old, has 18 holes meandering through beautiful forests with well-maintained and challenging fairways.

Alpine Resort
7670 Horseshoe Bay Rd., Egg Harbor, 888-281-8128
alpineresort.com

Peninsula State Park Golf Course
9890 N Shore Rd., Ephraim, 920-854-5791
peninsulagolf.org

MAKE IT A GOLF VACATION!

Door County has many courses for you to choose from.

The Orchards at Egg Harbor

8125 Heritage Lake Rd., Egg Harbor, 920-868-2483
orchardsateggharbor.com

Idlewild Golf Club

4146 Golf Valley Dr., Sturgeon Bay, 920-743-3334
idlewildgolfclub.com

Stone Hedge Golf and Pub

4320 County E, Egg Harbor, 920-868-1861
stonehedgegolfandpub.com

Cherry Hills Golf & Lodge

5905 Dunn Rd., Sturgeon Bay, 920-743-3240
golfcherryhills.com

Maxwelton Braes Golf Course

7670 WI-57, Baileys Harbor, 920-421-4653
golfmaxweltonbraes.com

27 Pines Golf Course

5611 Silverdale Rd., Sturgeon Bay, 920-746-8762
facebook.com/27pinesgolf

52

BE AWE-INSPIRED
AT CAVE POINT COUNTY PARK

While spectacular scenery is abundant throughout Door County, one spot is uniquely awe-inspiring. With wild natural elements, Cave Point County Park will truly take your breath away. Be mesmerized by Lake Michigan views from a perch several stories atop limestone and dolomite cliffs and ledges. Outcroppings and water-level caves below have been carved out and crafted by Lake Michigan waves. Varying locations along a walking path offer changing views of the cliffs and the caves.

When the lake is calm, the waters below are turquoise and pristine like a Caribbean Bay. When the lake is turbulent, large waves slam against the ledges and caves creating thunderous claps of sound and sending spray high in the air. Heading south on the trail, watch for blowholes, which in calm water provide a porthole to the lake below and in turbulent conditions can spray water upward as if you're standing atop a whale.

5360 Schauer Rd., Sturgeon Bay, 920-743-5511
co.door.wi.gov

TIP

If you want to add some hiking, the park includes a half-mile wooded trail. Or you can follow the lakeside path south, approximately a mile and a half, to Whitefish Dunes State Park. And for close-up water-level views that you won't get from the ledges above, explore the caves and coves by kayak! Yes! You will get to kayak into a cave. Kayak tours are available for paddlers of all levels.

Door County Kayak Tours
doorcountykayaktours.com

Peninsula Kayak Company
peninsulakayakcompany.com

Lakeshore Adventures Kayak Tours
doorcountykayaking.com/door-county-kayak-tour-info

53

HIT THE SNOWY TRAIL

All summer long, bikers and hikers are drawn to Door County's trails and shorelines, and its waters are dotted with boaters and paddlers. But in winter, the peninsula embraces a new season, Mother Nature takes a deep breath, and the fresh crisp weather offers unique outdoor experiences. Door County's forests, bluffs, fields, and waterways take on a majestic beauty, serenity, and tranquility when blanketed in snow.

Time to bust out the cross-country skis! Peninsula State Park, Potawatomi State Park, and Newport State Park are go-to destinations for groomed ski trails. Glide through quiet wintry forests and enjoy the park's magnificent views through a glistening snowy lens. If hiking is more your jam, give snowshoeing a try. Trek across snowy Door County landscapes or blaze new trails not available once the snow melts.

Cap your winter adventure hunkered down in front of a roaring fire.

Peninsula State Park
9462 Shore Rd., Fish Creek, 920-868-3258
dnr.wisconsin.gov/topic/parks/peninsula

Potawatomi State Park
3740 Bay Shore Dr., Sturgeon Bay, 920-746-2890
dnr.wisconsin.gov/topic/parks/potawatomi

Newport State Park
475 WI-42, Ellison Bay, 920-854-2500
dnr.wisconsin.gov/topic/parks/newport

TIP

Don't have your own gear? Cross-country ski and snowshoe rentals are available at various outfitters around the peninsula. Check out Bay Shore Outfitters or Nor Door Sport and Cyclery.

Bay Shore Outfitters

2457 S Bay Shore Dr., Sister Bay, 920-854-7598
bayshoreoutfitters.com

Nor Door Sport and Cyclery

4007 Hwy. 42, Fish Creek, 920-868-2275
nordoorsports.com

GO BOWLING
AT SISTER BAY BOWL

Your Door County adventure is probably focused on outdoor activities. But sometimes Mother Nature has a different plan in mind. Don't fear bad weather; go bowling! (Or seriously, go bowling in any weather because it's fun.)

Earl's Sister Bay Bowl and Supper Club is a family-friendly, six-lane bowling alley with a retro vibe that hearkens to the 1950s. Attached to the bowling alley are a supper club and neighborhood bar known for fish fry and old-fashioneds. This classic Sister Bay establishment has been owned and lovingly maintained by the same family for generations and is an active supporter of community events.

So book a lane or book the whole place! Enjoy bowling the way it was meant to be played, complete with manual score keeping and accompanied by good food and a Wisconsin beer or classic cocktail.

10640 N Bay Shore Dr., Sister Bay, 920-854-2841
sisterbaybowl.com

DO IT ALL
IN PENINSULA STATE PARK

Whatever outdoorsy thing you want to do, you can do it in Peninsula State Park: biking, hiking, camping, or golfing. This roughly four-acre state park boasts miles of shoreline. Park amenities include beaches, miles of trails, campsites, the Eagle Bluff Lighthouse, the Northern Sky Theater, and the Peninsula State Park Golf Course. The park features an impressive array of terrains and settings, from wooded trails to water access to rocky bluffs with spectacular views.

A popular park feature is Eagle Tower. A newly constructed lookout tower with an observation deck over 200 above the water, the tower offers impressive panoramic views. Climb the steps to get a little cardio with your sightseeing or take a leisurely and scenic stroll on the fully accessible "canopy walk."

9462 Shore Rd., Fish Creek, 920-868-3258
dnr.wisconsin.gov/topic/parks/peninsula

TIP

If you're not camping in the park or spending an afternoon on the trails, you can still enjoy the unique landscapes and vistas this spectacular park offers with a scenic drive through. Spot an eagle, gasp at a view, or catch a sunset. Pull-offs, scenic lookouts, and parking areas throughout the park offer magnificent views and a great adventure.

CATCH A BIG ONE

Whether it's the relaxation of a quiet afternoon casting a line in calm waters or the thrill of seeing your rod double over from a dauntingly large catch in the waves of Lake Michigan, Door County has your fishing aspirations covered! Between the waters of Lake Michigan and Green Bay, it's all here! Bass, walleye, salmon, muskie, and trout. Plus, the peninsula has many quality companies offering guides and tours for your expedition.

If you're a hearty soul angling to drop a line in the deep of winter, Door County is a great place to give ice fishing a try. If you've never gauged ice thickness or popped up an ice shanty on your own, guides are available.

Note: There is such an abundance of quality fishing tours and guides, we chose to not list any in these pages. An online search of "Door County Fishing" will help you find an expedition that's right for you.

TIP

For a fun, low-key fishing afternoon check out one of Door County's inland lakes. Bring your tackle box and a chair and cast a line in Kangaroo Lake off the County E causeway. Then follow it up with a beer and burger on the deck at Coyote Roadhouse on 3026 County Line Road E in Baileys Harbor.

920-839-9192
coyote-roadhouse.com

GET A BIRD'S-EYE VIEW
FROM ELLISON BLUFF

If heights give you heart palpitations, you might want to wait in the car, because the scenic overlook in Ellison Bluff County Park features an awe-inspiring bird's-eye view both *out* over Green Bay and *down* from the soaring bluff you are perched upon. The overlook is connected to the Ellison Bluff Loop, a well-maintained easy trail, under a mile long, that winds through beautiful woodlands. A short boardwalk structure at the overlook location leads you out along the edge of the bluffs for a breathtaking (or possibly frightening) view and impressive selfie backdrop.

This lookout is a lesser-known Door County gem. The rocky cliffs you are on top of are part of the Niagara Escarpment, and the county park is a great destination for a tranquil nature hike, picnic, sunset, or northern lights display.

12050 Ellison Bluff Rd., Liberty Grove, 608-266-2621
co.door.wi.gov/534/Ellison-Bluff-County-Park

TAKE THE SCALLYWAGS A-PUTTIN'

AT PIRATE'S COVE

Shiver me timbers! Despite the calm seas and vacation pirate booty being expended, yer wee lads and lasses can scuttle a vacay with midweek a-whinin' and complainin'. Take the little scallywags for an upliftin' whole-crew adventure at Pirate's Cove Adventure Golf!

Choose yer tiny club, yer colorful ball, and steady yer sea legs, as pirate ships, caves, and waterfalls lure ya in. But be warned: Pirate's Cove is not for the faint of heart. As you move from hole to hole, you will learn about pirate lore and the swashbucklers (men and women!) whose tales are bigger than the seven seas.

2502 S Bay Shore Dr., Sister Bay, 920-854-4929
piratescove.net

TIP

If the mateys aren't a-nappin' by the end of your Pirate's Cove adventure, visit Johnson's Park right next door for more mini-putting fun. Johnson's also features go-carts for all ages, batting cages, and a video arcade.

10611 N Highland Rd., Sister Bay, 920-421-2684
doorcountypulse.com/organization/johnsons-park

SLEEP UNDER THE STARS

If Door County's natural beauty makes you sad to head indoors at night, maybe you should be camping! For traditional campsites in beautiful settings, check out Peninsula State Park and Potawatomi State Park. These parks have facilities to accommodate all experience levels as well as a wide variety of amenities. Also, for winter enthusiasts, Peninsula State Park has year-round camping!

If you're willing to remove yourself from civilization by two ferry rides and a rugged hike to your campsite, Rock Island State Park is for you. Newport State Park also offers rustic, hike-in campsites, minus the ferry ride.

Maybe you prefer a family-friendly RV resort with a pool for the kiddos. You'll find campgrounds available across the peninsula. For a comprehensive listing visit: doorcounty.com/stay/campgrounds.

Peninsula State Park
9462 Shore Rd., Fish Creek, 920-868-3258
dnr.wisconsin.gov/topic/parks/peninsula

Potawatomi State Park
3740 Park Dr., Sturgeon Bay, 920-746-2890
dnr.wisconsin.gov/topic/parks/potawatomi

Rock Island State Park
1924 Indian Pt. Rd., Washington Island, 920-847-2235
dnr.wisconsin.gov/topic/parks/rockisland

Newport State Park
475 County Road NP, Ellison Bay, 920-854-2500
dnr.wisconsin.gov/topic/parks/newport

FLY HIGH ABOVE THE TREES
WITH ZIP-LINING

While you've admired Door County's natural beauty from land and by water, it may be time to do some sightseeing from a different perspective: that is if you can keep your eyes open as you zip along high above the treetops in a heart-pounding thrill ride. For spectacular views and perhaps a boost of adrenaline, go zip-lining!

Door County offers a variety of zip-lining options, from courses that accommodate all skill levels to high-flying canopy adventures for thrill seekers. Zip-line courses are located at different locations in forested areas of the peninsula giving you zippy views of nature preserves and Lake Michigan.

Get up out of that beach chair and prove to your friends that you're brave enough to fly high over the trees. Or show the kids that being outside and away from their phones can be a blast. Check out the courses and challenge options and call for a reservation.

Lakeshore Adventures Zip Line Tours
8113 WI-57, Baileys Harbor, 920-839-2055
lakeshore-adventures.com/zip-line-tours

Door County Adventure Center
4497 Ploor Rd., Sturgeon Bay, 920-746-9539
dcadventurecenter.com

61

STAY IN
MID-CENTURY STYLE

Two iconic Door County resorts feature early- to mid-20th-century glam, lush grounds, and ample amenities. Gordon Lodge, north of Baileys Harbor, and Alpine Lodge, south of Egg Harbor, are resorts that were built in the 1920s and occupy fabulous lakefront sites.

Both resorts have early 1900s Great Camp to 1940s/'50s mid-century vibes, have been tastefully renovated, and are meticulously maintained.

Gordon Lodge is nestled between deep woods and the Lake Michigan shoreline and features a beach, swimming pool, tennis courts, and hiking trails. Cozy cabins are available, but the resort's crowning feature is a cool, mid-century lodge. Alpine Resort enjoys an enviable lakefront setting and features classy cabins, a Great Camp–style lodge, manicured grounds, and a legendary golf course.

Gordon Lodge
1420 Pine Dr., Baileys Harbor, 920-839-2331
gordonlodge.com

Alpine Resort
7715 Alpine Rd., Egg Harbor, 920-868-3000
alpineresort.com

HIT THE ROAD
FOR A SCENIC DRIVE

With so much fun waiting to be had, where do you begin? The answer? Just go for a drive! Door County has such an abundance of amazing scenery, quaint establishments, and roadside attractions that car rides can actually be fun!

State Highways 42 and 57 loop the peninsula and make up the Door County Coastal Byway, one of only five official Scenic Byways in the state of Wisconsin.

On the east side of the peninsula are four officially designated Rustic Roads that run north from Sturgeon Bay along Lake Michigan. Washington Island is ringed by the fifth. Watch for brown and yellow signs identifying Rustic Roads.

Another fun drive is the curvy stretch of Highway 42 from Gills Rock to the tip of the peninsula. Some attribute the serpentine pattern to the influence of Jens Jensen, a famous landscape architect who established the Clearing Folk School in Ellison Bay in the 1930s.

Door County Coastal Byway
920-839-2288
doorcountycoastalbyway.org

Door County Rustic Roads
wisconsindot.gov/Pages/travel/road/rustic-roads/northeast.aspx

GAWK AT BOATS
(OR GO SAILING)

Nothing evokes a sense of freedom and adventure like a big boat. If you're not lucky enough to own (or have friends with) a massive yacht, big-masted sailboat, or fishing boat covered in gear, you can at least spend a day gawking at them. The villages dotting the coastlines have picturesque harbors full of impressive boats. Stroll the piers, don a captain's cap, and take a selfie. Begin your boat-gawking tour in Sturgeon Bay. Not only are there many marinas, but the commercial ships in the shipping canal will inspire the mariner in you.

Done gawking and ready to get out on the water yourself? Consider chartering an elegant sailboat or taking a tour with one of the peninsula's sailboat charter companies.

Sail Door County
10707 N Bay Shore Drive, Sister Bay, 920-495-7245
saildoorcounty.com

Bella Sailing Cruises
9993 State Hwy. 42, Ephraim, 920-854-2628
facebook.com/BellaSailingCruises

TIP

Sturgeon Bay has a rich history of shipbuilding, including yachts. An online search will provide you with stories of the shipbuilding companies that built Sturgeon Bay's economic development and culture.

64

PAMPER YOURSELF
WITH A SPA DAY

Spas are probably not the first thing that comes to mind when you think about Northern Wisconsin. But a spa visit is the perfect complement to the variety of activities available on the peninsula.

A deep tissue massage may be just what you need after a weekend of hiking, biking, and paddleboarding. Loosen up for your big golf outing or relax after kayaking with a shoulder massage. Schedule a luxurious facial treatment to get your glow on as you prep for a glamorous girls' outing of boutique shopping, gallery hopping, and fine dining. Or escape the kiddies and the busy family activities for a little private time.

Door County has three lovely spas offering a plethora of indulgent, relaxing, healing, and self-rewarding treatments. Each has a unique feel and focus so check out their websites to book your spa day or make it a spa vacation and visit all three!

The Spa at Sacred Grounds
10453 Townline Dr., Ephraim, 920-854-4733
sacredgroundsspa.com

Lavender Spa
9126 WI-42, Fish Creek, 920-868-3524
settlementinn.com/lavender-spa

Spa Verde Green Salon & Spa
7821 WI-42, Egg Harbor, 920-868-1597
spaverdesalon.com

SPOT PELICANS, EAGLES, AND EGRETS, OH MY!

To infuse an unplanned thrill into your adventure, pay attention to what's going on overhead and out over the water. You may just spot something truly breathtaking!

Bald eagles, once on the endangered species list, are alive and well and living in Door County. When you're out hiking or sightseeing, keep an eye turned skyward and you just might spot one soaring majestically along the shoreline looking for its lunch. Pelicans can be spotted traveling in little flotillas on waterways from the lake to the many bays and inland waters or flying in squadrons overhead. Egrets and other types of herons are frequently spotted not only as art subjects in galleries but also live, elegantly fishing in shallow waters.

For bird-watching in general, the Destination Door County website features maps of great spots across the peninsula.

doorcounty.com/experience/birding/birding-maps

TIP

Now that your bald eagle sighting has you excited to see more birds, head to the Open Door Bird Sanctuary at 4114 County I in Sturgeon Bay. ODB has interesting bird exhibits, including owls, hawks, and falcons, and offers demonstrations and presentations for avian education. The sanctuary also features hiking trails and picnic areas.

920-421-2684, doorcountypulse.com/organization/johnsons-park

Standing sentinel:
the Cana Island Lighthouse

CULTURE AND HISTORY

CLIMB TO THE TOP
OF THE CANA ISLAND LIGHTHOUSE

Looking out over Lake Michigan from a narrow walkway 80 feet in the air isn't for the faint of heart! But a visit to the Cana Island Lighthouse is a must for any Door County vacation. Built in 1869, the lighthouse is on the National Register of Historic Places and remains a functioning navigational light under the jurisdiction of the US Coast Guard. The restored caretaker's house, outbuildings, and educational displays offer a glimpse of the critical job and desolate life of a lighthouse keeper.

The big fun is climbing the tower! Ninety-seven filigree iron steps take you on a tight, twisty trek to the top. The climb is a challenge and includes a tight tuck and squeeze into the watch room at the top. But the spectacular views and opportunity to see the Fresnel lens up close makes the climb worth the effort.

8800 E Cana Island Rd., Baileys Harbor, 920-743-5958
dcmm.org/cana-island-lighthouse

TIP

The lighthouse visit fun begins upon arrival. With varying lake levels, the approximately 400-foot-long causeway leading to Cana Island can be either underwater or a dry, rocky, gravely path. You can walk (or wade!) but the walk can be challenging and ankle-turning, and wading can be cold and (obviously) wet. Rides in a tractor-pulled wagon are available to get you across the causeway.

TOUR THE HISTORIC
ALEXANDER NOBLE HOUSE

While you're busy shopping and looking for a place to eat in Fish Creek, you may notice, smack-dab on its busiest corner, a lovely historic white house with a big front porch. On the National Register of Historic Places, this was the home of Alexander Noble, considered one of Fish Creek's founding fathers. The history of the house is celebrated due to Mr. Noble's significance in the community and for being the first residential structure that wasn't a log home. The house was built in the late 1800s, and the architecture is considered a Greek Revival style. In addition, the museum features exhibits that offer a glimpse of different aspects of life during this time period.

Take a break from shopping and add to the Fish Creek fun with a tour of this unique Door County museum. Self-guided audio tours and docent-led tours are available.

4167 Hwy. 42, Fish Creek, 920-868-2091
historicnoble.org

TIP

Bonus! It's supposedly haunted. Watch for weird stuff while on your tour or hop aboard a Door County Trolley's Ghost Tour. (Door County Trolley has several haunted tours. Ask for the tour that includes the Alexander Noble House.)

doorcountytrolley.com

GET THEE TO
DOOR SHAKESPEARE

"One touch of nature makes the whole world kin." – Shakespeare

Students of Shakespeare will surely point out that this quote is referring to human nature, not Mother Nature. However, on its surface it describes the conviviality of attending a Door Shakespeare production and the influence of its beautiful natural setting. This open-air theater is nestled in the woods next to Lake Michigan on the grounds of Björklunden.

The unassuming stage wraps around an enormous tree, and audiences are transported through clever set designs. The seating hugs the stage for an intimate theatrical experience, and the actors often engage or blend into the audience creating a companionable spirit among the enthusiastic crowd. The talented, professional actors bring to life the timeless tales of the Bard with unique staging and interpretation. Check out their website for special events such as preshow catered dinners, programs, and Camp Will, a theater camp for kids.

Door Shakespeare
Daytime Box Office
10038 WI-57, Sister Bay

Theater (Björklunden)
7590 Boynton Ln.
Baileys Harbor, 920-854-7111
doorshakespeare.com

IMMERSE YOURSELF IN ART
AT EDGEWOOD ORCHARD GALLERIES

Door County is known not only for its natural beauty but also as a visual arts destination. Combine a stroll through nature with an immersion in art at the Edgewood Orchard Galleries' sculpture garden. Wind along wooded paths lined with sculptures crafted from metals and other materials. The beautiful, natural setting creates a dramatic backdrop for the art, some of it impressively large, some small and detailed, all of it stunning and beautiful.

When you've completed your tour of the gardens, spend some time in the galleries. Located in a beautifully restored barn brimming with color and art pieces and surrounded by lush landscape, this highly regarded gallery features the diverse work of many established, respected artists. Edgewood hosts occasional opening events, artist introductions and talks, and exciting group shows. After Thanksgiving, the gallery has weekend holiday shows filled with festive spirit and the opportunity to find unique artsy gifts.

4140 Peninsula Players Rd., Fish Creek, 920-868-3579
edgewoodorchard.com

EXPLORE NAUTICAL HISTORY AT DOOR COUNTY MARITIME MUSEUM

A trip to Door County brings out the hearty ship captain or moody lighthouse keeper in all of us. When you get bitten by the nautical bug and crave a little backstory to all the nautical feels, a trip to the Maritime Museum is a must.

Sturgeon Bay has a busy working waterfront thanks to the Sturgeon Bay Ship Canal that connects the Bay of Green Bay with Lake Michigan. Located in the middle of everything is the Maritime Museum showcasing the region's rich maritime history, including backstories on some of the hundreds of shipwrecks that surround the peninsula. Also, the museum features a restored 1919 tugboat called the *John Purves*, a tour of which lets you experience the life of a tugboat crewman, and the Jim Kress Maritime Lighthouse Tower featuring imagination-inspiring exhibits related to the region's nautical heritage.

Hearty ship captains and moody lighthouse keepers get hungry. Follow your museum visit with a hearty meal at one of Sturgeon Bay's unique restaurants (sturgeonbay.net/dine).

120 N Madison Ave., Sturgeon Bay, 920-743-5958
dcmm.org

TIP

Boat enthusiasts will enjoy the Door County Classic and Wooden Boat Show held in early August. The museum grounds and waterfront are the backdrop for a showcase of beautifully crafted or restored wooden boats and other interesting things that float. This event is held during Sturgeon Bay's Maritime Week.

DISCOVER
DIVERSE ECOSYSTEMS AT THE RIDGES SANCTUARY

The Ridges Sanctuary is a nature enthusiasts' dream as well as a great place to hike or enjoy an educational family outing. Founded in the 1930s, the Ridges protects acres of diverse ecosystems. The name comes from the ridges of land that formed as the Lake Michigan shoreline receded over centuries. The ridges run parallel to the lake from the lower elevation of today's lake shore to the higher elevation from centuries ago. Between the ridges are swales (think shallow channels) that create wetlands and marshes. With different elevations and proximity to the lake, each ridge and swale features a unique ecosystem with varying forests, plants, wildflowers, and wildlife.

Well-marked and maintained walking paths follow the ridges and boardwalks cross the swales. The modern visitors' center provides educational materials, and the grounds include a Family Discovery Trail to engage your little ones.

8166 State Highway 57, Baileys Harbor, 920-839-2802
ridgessanctuary.org

TIP

The Ridges Sanctuary is also home to the Baileys Harbor Range Lights, a unique type of lighthouse used to alert ships to the dangers of shallow waters around Baileys Harbor. Tours are available.

DON'T FEAR

THE DEATH'S DOOR MARITIME MUSEUM

While getting your sea legs with a deep dive into Door County's nautical history, be sure to include a visit to Death's Door Maritime Museum in Gills Rock. The scary name references the navigational passage connecting Lake Michigan and Green Bay between the peninsula and Washington Island, which is known as a dangerous strait responsible for many of the region's shipwrecks.

While not as big as the Door County Maritime Museum in Sturgeon Bay, this museum packs a punch with exhibits on the history of Death's Door and the region's commercial fishing. In addition to loads of fishing industry paraphernalia, the museum features a wooden fishing tugboat dating from the 1930s called *Hope*. Visitors can explore the boat and learn about its history. The museum also has an exhibit featuring interesting artifacts retrieved from deep in the Lake Michigan waters and from various shipwreck sites.

12724 W Wisconsin Bay Rd., Ellison Bay, 920-743-5958
dcmm.org/deaths-door-maritime-museum

TIP

Head just down the street to the Shoreline Restaurant for a great seafood dinner and stunning views of Green Bay.

12747 WI 42, Ellison Bay, 920-854-2950
theshorelinerestaurant.com

GLIMPSE THE PAST
IN HISTORIC SETTINGS

How did people live before cars, cell phones, and Netflix? Door County enthusiasts, history buffs, and anyone curious about rural life over a decade ago will love visiting two historic sites. These interesting destinations capture life in rural northern Wisconsin from post–Civil War through the early 1900s.

Heritage Village at Big Creek includes restored buildings that housed critical community services and businesses appropriate to the region and its agricultural roots. Buildings include a school, store, chapel, and more. Some buildings, such as the blacksmith shop, offer active demonstrations of the trade it housed.

Corner of the Past Museum features the Old Anderson House Museum, a post–Civil War farmhouse with architectural features unique to the era. Additional restored buildings representative of a working farm offer a glimpse into rural life on the peninsula during this era. Buildings include a sawmill, summer kitchen, and additional historic residential and vacation cottages.

Heritage Village at Big Creek
2041 Michigan Ave., Sturgeon Bay, 920-421-2332
doorcountyhistoricalsociety.org/heritage-village

Corner of the Past Museum
10310 Fieldcrest Rd., Sister Bay, 920-854-7680
sisterbayhistory.org/museum

TIP

The museum grounds at Corner of the Past Museum are also the site of a weekly Saturday-morning farmers market in summer and fall months. In November and December, the grounds transform into a holiday wonderland as the site of the popular Christkindlmarkt.

doorcountychristmasmarket.com

74

BE DAZZLED
AT PENINSULA PLAYERS THEATER

For a truly dazzling Door County evening, attend a performance at Peninsula Players Theater. The magic starts when you arrive at the theater, which is located in a beautiful setting on the shores of Green Bay and is referred to as the "Theatre in a Garden." Landscaped paths lead you through the forest toward festive lighting. You can wait for your show to start at a deep-woods beer garden with sunset views over the Bay. The updated theater is rustic and woodsy, yet gloriously open-air with large windows along the sidewalls.

Peninsula Players performs plays in a variety of genres including modern playwrights, classic comedies, or perhaps an Agatha Christie mystery. Also, Peninsula Players is a resident company! Everyone involved in the show, from actors to administrators, lives on the property. In fact, Peninsula Players is considered America's oldest resident summer theater.

4351 Peninsula Players Rd., Fish Creek, 920-868-3287
peninsulaplayers.com

UNLEASH YOUR CREATIVITY AT PENINSULA SCHOOL OF ART

While vacationing in Door County, it's fun to gallery-hop, attend exhibits, and buy art for your personal collection. But it's much more fun and rewarding to be a creator. Budding and seasoned artists alike can unleash their talents at the Peninsula School of Art. For decades, PenArt has provided the peninsula with art classes, events for kids, seminars and talks, studio space and residencies, exhibitions, and the popular Plein Air Festival.

This exciting facility is on an expansive campus in Fish Creek. The building includes classrooms, studio space, and the Guenzel Gallery, an exhibition space in a historic round barn. Studios include spaces for painting, jewelry making, metal arts, ceramics, and more. The grounds include public sculpture and other art.

So, tour the beautiful grounds, explore the sculptures on display, attend an exhibit, or better yet, sign up for a class or studio time and unleash your creativity.

Peninsula School of Art
3900 County F, Fish Creek, 920-868-3455
peninsulaschoolofart.org

Guenzel Gallery
peninsulaschoolofart.org/guenzel-gallery

WALK IN THE SHOES
OF AN EAGLE BLUFF LIGHTHOUSE KEEPER

Has there ever been a more critical job than that of a lighthouse keeper tasked with keeping a light functioning 24/7 to guide ships and crews through treacherous waters? A tour of Eagle Bluff Lighthouse gives background and insight on what life was like for these hearty souls as well as the families stuck in that lighthouse with them.

Eagle Bluff is a functioning lighthouse, operated by the US Coast Guard, and is on the National Register of Historic Places. Perched on a bluff high above the water in Peninsula State Park, this lighthouse guides boats through the Strawberry Channel. The grounds are free to explore, and a tour of the building is well worth the cost of admission to hear stories about the actual keepers who manned the light over a century ago. The keeper's residence includes some original furnishings and antiques from the era.

10249 Shore Rd., Fish Creek, 920-421-2332
doorcountyhistoricalsociety.org/eagle-bluff-lighthouse

TIP

After climbing to the top of Cana Island Lighthouse and exploring the lovely grounds of Eagle Bluff Lighthouse, you may find yourself obsessing over these unique structures. If only you could get a closer look at the other storied lighthouses. With the Door Peninsula Lighthouse Festivals, you can!

During the festival, held twice a year in the spring and fall, lighthouses that are not normally accessible to the public are available to explore, including lighthouses on the peninsula and in neighboring communities. You can sign up for hiking tours, kayak tours, boat tours, and tours by plane! The lighthouses included in the festival can vary from year to year, and different sites have unique arrangements for access, so research is required.

Door Peninsula Lighthouse Festivals

dcmm.org/door-county-lighthouse-festivals

ADMIRE A PAINTER AT WORK

IN PLEIN AIR

Plein air painting is the practice of getting outside of the studio and into nature. While the history of plein air painting includes artists of different centuries, continents, and styles, it is notable in French Impressionism. A significant feature is capturing the impact of light on the landscape.

In late July, Door County's fine-arts culture and natural beauty converge for an art lover's dream event, the Plein Air Festival. More than 30 artists selected from around the country spend a week painting in open-air sites around the peninsula. If you're out exploring Door County during this event, watch for an artist behind an easel busy at work capturing a gorgeous landscape or iconic Door County image.

Plein Air includes lectures and hands-on activities for the whole family. Or purchase a "Palette Pass" that gives access to a range of events including the chance to purchase or bid on the art created during Plein Air.

Peninsula School of Art, 3900 County F, Fish Creek, 920-868-3455
peninsulaschoolofart.org/doorcountypleinair

TIP

If you enjoy seasonal local celebrations that offer a deeper dive into the culture and vibe, check the websites of the various villages, doorcounty.com, or doorcountypulse.com to find something fun happening during your visit. Two faves are Ephraim's early spring Fyr Bal "Door County meets Burning Man" and Sister Bay's New Year's Eve Cherry Drop "Door County meets Times Square."

LEARNING IS FUN
AT THE FARM

Baby goats, piglets, and chicks! No better way to entertain the wee ones than with cute and cuddly animals. The Farm, just north of Sturgeon Bay, delivers in the adorable-animal department. However, there's so much more!

On its website, The Farm is referred to as a "living museum of rural America." The grounds include modern barns and historic structures, as well as trails, gardens, and crop fields. Learning sneaks in disguised as fun in categories such as agricultural history, farming, and ecology. Discover the use of antique tools, try your hand at milking a goat, and watch chicks being born.

Despite all that fun (and sneaky learning), the big draw is those crazy-cute baby animals, and the main event is feeding them with a bottle. Throw in your own cute kids (human, not goat) and you are guaranteed a phone full of adorable photos with which to impress your friends.

4285 WI-57, Sturgeon Bay, 920-743-6666
thefarmindoorcounty.com

LEAVE YOUR MARK
AT ANDERSON DOCK

Bring your paintbrush (but no spray paint, please) to make your mark at Anderson Dock in Ephraim. The historic warehouse on this dock is known for its graffitied wood siding. Historically, boaters signed the exterior walls of the warehouse with the name of their boat and the year they visited. Now all are encouraged to leave their mark, keeping it tasteful and without carving into the wood.

The whole site is an interesting visual juxtaposition with the vibrant and colorful graffitied warehouse set against the nautical look of the dock with the picturesque Village of Ephraim and Eagle Harbor in the background.

Adding to that mix is the Hardy Gallery that occupies the warehouse. Hardy is a popular fine-arts gallery with exciting exhibits, featuring established and new artists, both regional and national.

Anderson Dock
3083 Anderson Ln., Ephraim
ephraim.wi.gov/visiting-anderson-dock

Hardy Gallery
3083 Anderson Ln., Ephraim
thehardy.org

LEARN SOMETHING UNEXPECTED
AT BJÖRKLUNDEN

Return from your Door County vacation relaxed, tan, and . . . smarter?! Björklunden, part of Lawrence University, is a retreat nestled in the woods near the Lake Michigan shoreline that offers weeklong seminars in a vast range of topics. Take a deep dive into history, politics, or philosophy. Expand your knowledge of film or theater. Learn about mushrooms or birch trees or the night sky. Or develop your inner artist with watercolor or digital photography.

The facility is a rustic, Scandinavian-style lodge that contains classrooms, seminar spaces, and guest rooms. The peaceful grounds also house the Door Shakespeare theater and the Boynton Chapel, a historic Stavkirke structure.

As their website states, the classes provide "vacations with a purpose." Check out Björklunden's seminar schedule, register for something you're curious to learn about, then impress your friends and neighbors with what you learned on your summer vacation.

7590 Boynton Ln., Baileys Harbor, 920-839-2216
lawrence.edu/bjorklunden

TIP

For a totally immersive experience, you can stay at Björklunden during your seminar or just include a daily afternoon class as part of your Door County vacation.

SUPPORT SUSTAINABLE STEWARDSHIP
AT HORSESHOE BAY FARMS

Door County has a way of seeping into your soul. Enthusiasts return year after year and share a deep yearning to protect the peninsula for the good of the planet and the enjoyment of future generations.

Horseshoe Bay Farms is referred to as "A Center for Sustainable Stewardship" offering both a glimpse of the past and a vision for the future. From its earliest roots as the Horseshoe Bay Settlement, a lumber town in the late 1800s, to Horseshoe Bay Farms, one of the largest fruit producers and employers in the county, this farm has played a significant role in the history and culture of Egg Harbor. Today you can tour historic barns and gardens and learn about this nonprofit's vision for a sustainable future.

7212 Horseshoe Bay Rd., Egg Harbor, 920-495-9988
horseshoebayfarms.org

TIP

Horseshoe Bay Farms features *Stickwork*, an original art installation by Patrick Dougherty, a renowned artist who combines sculpture with nature by creating large interactive structures out of tree saplings.

stickwork.net

RELEASE YOUR INNER NOVELIST
AT WRITE ON, DOOR COUNTY

Is there a novel or memoir knocking around in your head? Do you dream of seeing your name on the cover of a book? Aspiring writers and enthusiastic readers alike will find inspiration and celebrate the written word at Write On, Door County. Located in its stunning new Writing Center in Fish Creek, Write On offers an extensive schedule of activities and events such as classes, seminars, and author and poet readings. Writers can participate in full writing retreats, including the Washington Island Literary Festival, or can apply for a residency for a dedicated writing experience. Write On often teams with other arts organizations for events designed to encourage creative writing inspired by music or visual arts. The facility's beautiful grounds inspire creativity as well. Ponder prose on the 1.5-mile Writer's Walk or enjoy quiet and focused reading time with a Readers' Café.

4210 Juddville Rd., Fish Creek, 920-868-1457
writeondoorcounty.org

83

ENGAGE IN THE ARTS
IN STURGEON BAY

Make sure your Door County arts indulgence includes a visit to the city of Sturgeon Bay. The Miller Art Museum (MAM), Door County's only fine-arts museum, houses a large permanent collection of works by 20th-century Wisconsin and Midwest artists and of its founder, artist Gerhard C.F. Miller. MAM joins 12 other museums, including the Madison Museum of Contemporary Art and Milwaukee Art Museum, as designated Wisconsin Art Destinations, organizations working together to raise the profile of Wisconsin as a visual arts destination.

Sturgeon Bay also delivers in performance art. Plan to attend performances at Third Avenue PlayWorks (TAP) and Rogue Theater. TAP is a performing-arts venue on historic Third Avenue featuring plays and musicals in a variety of genres. Rogue Theater presents community-theater performances in its new facility, DC Arts Center.

The Miller Art Museum
107 S 4th Ave., Sturgeon Bay
920-746-0707
millerartmuseum.org

Third Avenue PlayWorks
239 N 3rd Ave., Sturgeon Bay
920-743-1760
thirdavenueplayworks.org

Rogue Theater/DC Arts Center
917 N 14th Ave., Sturgeon Bay, 920-818-0816
roguetheater.org

ADMIRE A NORWEGIAN STAVE CHAPEL

Architecture buffs and enthusiasts of historic churches will be inspired by two stave churches in Door County. This Norwegian style of church architecture is predominantly constructed of wood poles, and in Norway some structures date back over 700 years.

Washington Island is home to the Stavkirke. While it is inspired by the historic Norwegian stave style, it was built in the 1980s in honor of the region's Scandinavian heritage. The Stavkirke is a beautiful chapel with a wood facade, a multitiered roof, a bell tower, and intricately carved wood ornamentation. The chapel is open to explore most days and hosts church services during summer months.

The Boynton Chapel is a stave church located on the grounds of Björklunden in Baileys Harbor. This historic structure was built in the 1940s and is a popular tourist spot. The building boasts hand-painted frescoes and intricately carved furnishings.

The Stavkirke
1763 Town Line Rd., Washington Island, 920-847-2341
washingtonisland.com/stavkirke

The Boynton Chapel
7590 Boynton Ln., Baileys Harbor, 920-839-2216
lawrence.edu/bjorklunden/boynton-chapel

AWAKEN YOUR CREATIVITY
AT THE CLEARING

Your creativity will flow and your soul will sing when you explore a new talent or hobby at the Clearing. Imagine an inspirational week of art, music, craft, humanities, or exploration inspired by the stunning natural beauty all around you, or explore a new interest with a single-day workshop. To further immerse yourself in the experience, consider staying on campus in a cozy cabin and forging bonds with your fellow learners over family-style meals. The large, wooded campus extends to the water's edge of Ellison Bay on the bluffs of the Niagara Escarpment.

The Clearing provides educational programs in what is referred to as a "folk school tradition," where learning is non-competitive, hands-on, and involves conversation, discussion, and nature study. The school was founded in the 1930s by Jens Jensen, a highly respected, Chicago-based landscape architect originally from Denmark. His influence and vision live on through the stunning architecture, lush setting, and spirit of communal learning.

12171 Garrett Bay Rd., Ellison Bay, 920-854-4088
theclearing.org

86

FIND INSPIRATION
AT WOODWALK GALLERY

When exploring Door County galleries, the itinerary must include the Woodwalk Gallery. Just south of Egg Harbor, this multifunctioning gallery truly embodies the peninsula's culture and arts vibe. Plan to dedicate extra time as Woodwalk features the diverse work of close to 100 artists. The vast array of art mediums and techniques ensure everyone will find a piece of work that captures their fancy or a style that inspires their own artistic aspirations.

Woodwalk occupies an exquisitely renovated barn with well-appointed gallery spaces, cool lighting, and interesting architecture that also serves as an arts center and event space. Catch an exhibit opening, attend a workshop, or participate in a farm-to-table dining experience. With the barn's desirable acoustics and ample space, Woodwalk also hosts live music featuring local musicians and national acts in a variety of genres including classical, chamber, folk, and more.

6746 County Rd. G, Egg Harbor, 920-629-4877
woodwalkgallery.com

Shopping in Sister Bay's exciting downtown

SHOPPING AND FASHION

SHOP TILL YOU DROP

You most likely drove to Door County, and that's a good thing. If shopping is on the itinerary, you'd never fit all those shopping bags in an airplane's overhead bin.

The villages that dot the western shore of the peninsula are a shopping enthusiast's dream destination. Egg Harbor, Fish Creek, Ephraim, and Sister Bay all have quaint but bustling downtowns brimming with unique shops. Boutiques with distinctive clothing and jewelry abound. Foodies and cooks will find specialty foods, farm markets, and cool kitchen gadgets. Art galleries and gift shops ensure you won't go home empty handed. Unique shops of all kinds—sporting goods, New Age paraphernalia, home goods, toys, and antiques—provide something for every interest. And of course, Door County swag and fun stuff is everywhere. So, pick a town, park the car, and stroll from end to end, store to store. The shopping stretches between towns as well for miles of retail therapy.

eggharbordoorcounty.org/shop

visitfishcreek.com/shop

ephraim-doorcounty.com/shop

sisterbay.com/shop

GEAR UP!

Kayaking! Biking! Snowshoeing! Fishing! With all the fun to be had across Door County, you're going to need some gear. These outstanding sports outfitters can suit you up for whatever you need for your Door County adventure.

Bay Shore Outfitters has locations in Sturgeon Bay and Sister Bay and can deliver on a wide variety of sports. Rent kayaks and stand-up paddleboards, electric bikes, and winter gear for cross-country skiing and snowshoeing. Bay Shore is also a go-to for camping needs.

Lakeshore Adventures in Baileys Harbor rents kayaks and stand-up paddleboards. Lakeshore can also set you up with fishing gear and boat rentals! (Pontoon ride, anyone?)

Nor Door Sport and Cyclery is conveniently located at the entry to Peninsula State Park in Fish Creek. Grab your gear, summer or winter, bikes or skis, and hit the park's trails.

Bay Shore Outfitters
2457 S Bay Shore Dr., Sister Bay, 920-854-7598
59 N Madison Ave., Sturgeon Bay, 920-818-0431
bayshoreoutfitters.com

Lakeshore Adventures
8113 WI-57, Baileys Harbor, 920-839-2055
lakeshore-adventures.com/store

Nor Door Sport and Cyclery
4007 Hwy. 42, Fish Creek, 920-868-2275
nordoorsports.com

GRAB YOUR DC MERCH
AT BEACH PEOPLE

For all your Door County merch or vacation swag, visit Beach People. Once you wander into this enticing, beachy, and colorful store, you will quickly discover that this is not a typical souvenir shop.

Beach People is the go-to destination for "Door County" emblazoned T-shirts and sweats or cozy throw blankets and beach towels. Indulge the little ones with toys and the teens with fun jewelry. Find great souvenirs like beer glasses, flip-flops, ornaments, soaps, and stickers. This gem of a store also features fun and tasteful accessories for your home—all with a Door County—themed, beach-life vibe.

With so much fun stuff to look at, it's sometimes hard to get out of the store. But you will leave happy with a great new sweatshirt or enough nautical decor to turn your home into a dreamy beach house.

9930 Hwy. 42, Ephraim, 920-854-7757
4201 Main St., Fish Creek, 920-868-4400
beachpeopledc.com

TIP

If Northwoods Wisconsin is more your style, visit their sister store, Lake People, in Fish Creek. Same great stuff as Beach People, just more bears and less fish!

Lake People

4201 Main St., Fish Creek, 920-868-4401
visitfishcreek.com/directory/lake-people-fish-creek

GO GALLERY-HOPPING

Door County is known for impressive natural wonders and quaint villages, and offers robust outdoor activities, restaurants, shops, lighthouses, and nautical history. But one of its most surprising charms is its hip, world-class visual arts scene. Whether drawn by the muse of the beautiful scenery or inspired by the well-established arts community, artists have been flocking to Door County for over a century.

Galleries are abundant, embellishing the villages and dotting the county roads, and showcasing impressive varieties of artists and techniques. Spend a day (or a full week!) infused in color and texture, find inspiration for your gallery wall, or leave Door County with the classiest of souvenirs: a piece of art. Map out a gallery-hopping itinerary but be ready to hit the brakes when something unexpected catches your eye. A great place to start is Plum Bottom Gallery. Colorful and fun, Plum Bottom features a wide range of artists, art pieces, and gifts.

4999 Plum Bottom Rd., Egg Harbor
7813 WI-42, Egg Harbor
4175 Main St., Fish Creek
231 N 3rd Ave., Sturgeon Bay
920-393-7885
plumbottomgallery.com

POPULAR GALLERIES

This partial list is a starting point leading you to discover additional exciting galleries.

Cappaert Contemporary Gallery

7901 WI-42, Egg Harbor, 920-868-3987
cappaertcontemporary.com

Popelka Trenchard Glass

64 S 2nd Ave., Sturgeon Bay, 920-743-7287
popelkaglass.com

Margaret Lockwood Gallery

7 S 2nd Ave., Sturgeon Bay, 920-493-3635
margaretlockwoodgallery.com

Idea Gallery

6551 County T, Egg Harbor, 920-655-1340
ideagalleryart.com

Fine Line Design Gallery & Sculpture Garden

10376 WI-42, Sister Bay, 920-854-4343
finelinedesignsgallery.com

Francis Hardy Gallery

The Anderson Warehouse, Ephraim, 920-854-2210
thehardy.org

Frykman Studio Gallery

2566 S Bay Shore Dr., Sister Bay, 920-854-7351
door-county-photography.com

M. Anderson Gallery

44 S 2nd Ave., Sturgeon Bay, 920-765-1332
mandersongallery.com

FIND SOMETHING TO READ

Looking for something to read poolside (or at the beach or in the hammock or in front of the fire)? Happily, you can find a book that will enhance your vacation chill at one of the charming independent bookstores on the peninsula.

Lion's Mouth Bookstore is in the heart of downtown Egg Harbor. This cozy little shop carries new and used titles. Browse a little, then take your new book next door and enjoy a cup of coffee at Big Easy.

The Peninsula Bookman just north of Fish Creek in Barringer Crossing carries a large collection of new and used books. Pick out a new book and stroll down the street to Fish Creek Beach.

Novel Bay Booksellers is an independent woman-owned shop in a sweet storefront on historic Third Avenue in Sturgeon Bay. Follow them on Facebook for author events and more.

Lion's Mouth Bookstore
7755 WI-42, Egg Harbor, 920-328-5523
lionsmouthbookstore.com

The Peninsula Bookman
4083 Main St., Fish Creek, 920-868-1467
peninsulabookman.com

Novel Bay Booksellers
44 N 3rd Ave., Sturgeon Bay, 920-365-9281
novelbaybooks.com

BE INFUSED
AT FRAGRANT ISLE LAVENDER FARM AND SHOP

A ferry ride to Washington Island delivers many delightful destinations to explore. But no trip to the island would be complete without a visit to the Fragrant Isle Lavender Farm and Shop. From the aromatic scent wafting on Lake Michigan breezes to the purple-hued landscape evocative of an impressionist painting, Fragrant Isle will intoxicate your senses. Fragrant Isle boasts being the largest single-site lavender grower in the Midwest and manages its farm with a deep appreciation and respect for its lavender plants, the environment, and the Washington Island community.

Start your visit with a tour of the farm and essential oil distillery. Follow the tour with lunch or a snack at Le Café. Enjoy a lavender-infused dessert, coffee drink, or lemonade. Or enjoy the beauty of the farm with a lavender-infused wine or cocktail. Wrap up your experience with a visit to the Fragrant Isle Retail Store or simply roam the beautiful fields and pick your own bundle of lavender.

1350 Airport Rd., Washington Island, 920-847-2950
fragrantisle.com

SPEND THE DAY
IN STURGEON BAY

For a satisfying hit of shopping dopamine, head to downtown Sturgeon Bay's historic Third Avenue. This charming area boasts a variety of unique shops and galleries along several easily navigable blocks.

Start your shopping bonanza at The Marketplace, a collection of exciting retailers selling fashion, furniture, home goods, and gifts. These distinctive shops operate from a large and airy open space within a renovated historic building—appropriately, a former department store. Then meander up and down Third Avenue for boutiques, art, kitchen accessories, New Age gifts, and more. Don't forget to check out the side streets along the way. When you're done hoofing it, get in the car and expand your tour. More delightful retailers can be found heading northeast along Jefferson Street and southwest across the Ship Canal. As you stroll the quaint downtown, one of Sturgeon Bay's many restaurants and eateries will surely catch your eye for a post-shopping bite to eat.

sturgeonbay.net/shop

sturgeonbay.net/dine

The Marketplace
58 N 3rd Ave., Sturgeon Bay, 920-743-6722
blissdoorcounty.com

FIND EVERYTHING DOOR COUNTY

AT LAUTENBACH'S

Sometimes a farm market can be a destination unto itself. Lautenbach's Orchard Country Winery & Market is one of those destinations: the embodiment of everything wonderfully Door County. If you're buzzing by on Highway 42, you might think, *Hmm, there's a cute farm store*. But don't be fooled. This place has much more than meets the driving-by eye.

The market in front contains a dizzying array of farm-market and specialty foods, artisan cheeses, seasonal fruit products, and a bakery with freshly baked seasonal goodies. Behind the store is the "rustic cupola room" (or bar!) where you can sample wines and ciders. Make an event out of your visit with food options and wine tastings, live music during summer months, and private wine tours. Or visit Lautenbach's as part of the Door County Wine Trail. Come with the whole family for cherry or apple picking (when in season) or test your skills at cherry-pit spitting.

9197 WI-42, Fish Creek, 920-868-3479
orchardcountry.com

BE UNIQUE
AND SHOP A BOUTIQUE

Has clicking through web pages of mediocrity left you feeling uninspired? Do you miss the days when shopping was fun and shopping bags were fancy? Good news! You're on vacation, and you've left the laptop behind. Time to go shopping, live and in person. Remember the joys of actually touching the clothing and trying things on?

Door County delivers that joy with an abundance of unique shops featuring distinctive clothing and accessories. With so many boutiques, everyone in your entourage, from girlfriend to grandma, will find a shop or perhaps a new outfit they like, and every style and taste will be accommodated: hip, trendy, casual, athletic, beachy . . . you name it.

The following page has an extra list of shops to get you started, but we recommend you keep a little notepad in your purse and jot down all the cool stores you pass as you're exploring the peninsula. Start your boutique crawl in Egg Harbor with two fun and fashion-forward shops, Spot and Blacksmith Clothing Co.

Spot
7775 WI-42, Egg Harbor
10647 N Bay Shore Dr., Sister Bay, 920-857-6862
spot.clothing

Blacksmith Clothing Co.
7806 Horseshoe Bay Rd., Egg Harbor, 920-868-3216
blacksmithclothingco.com

Ecology

10740 N Bay Shore Dr.
Sister Bay, 920-854-5724
ecologysports.com

Blue Ivy

9423 Spruce St., #3
Fish Creek, 920-868-5212
blueivyboutique.com

Patricia Shoppe

7681 WI-42, Egg Harbor
920-868-1537
patriciashoppe.com

Spruce Boutique

4152 Main St., Unit D
Fish Creek, 920-868-5077
spruceboutique.shop

Lilly Lo Boutique

9428 Cedar Ct., Ste. 10
Fish Creek, 920-660-1867
lillyloboutiques.com

Hide Side Boutique

4153 WI-42, Fish Creek
920-868-2665
hideside.com/hide-side-boutique

Camilla's

12033 WI-42, Ellison Bay
920-421-3718
camillasdc.com

Turtle Ridge Gallery

11736 Mink River Rd.
Ellison Bay, 920-854-4839
turtleridgegallery.com

Fred & Co.

4143 Main St., Fish Creek
920-868-2338
shopfred.com

Wink Swim Wear

4160 Main St., Fish Creek
920-868-3201
winkswimwear.com

O'Meara's Irish House

3970 Hwy. 42, Fish Creek
920-868-3528
omearasirish.com

On Deck Clothing Company

265 N 3rd Ave., Sturgeon Bay, 920-743-8778
ondeckclothing.com

Wilkins & Olander

120 N 3rd Ave., Sturgeon Bay
920-743-3137
wilkinsandolander.com

SHOP CHRISTMAS
YEAR ROUND

It may be your summer vacation, but Christmas is just around the corner! For those of you who love Christmas decorating and are always scouting out that next ornament or tabletop Santa, Door County has two magical, North Pole–worthy, Christmas destinations: Tannenbaum Holiday Shop and Mistletoe Holiday House.

You'll forget that it's 85 degrees outside when you enter rooms full of ornament-laden Christmas trees with a background soundtrack of holiday music and the scent of cinnamon and gingerbread. Add to your ornament collection, find inspiration for a new tree theme, pick up a unique Advent calendar, or snag a Christmas-themed souvenir. These lovely stores are a ho-ho-ho of a good time.

Tannenbaum Holiday Shop
11054 WI-42, Sister Bay, 920-854-5004
tannenbaumholidayshop.com

Mistletoe Holiday House
5135 Holiday Dr., Egg Harbor, 920-980-6834
mistletoe-holidayhouse.com

TREAT YOUR NOGGIN
AT HAT HEAD

If you want something for your head, you can find it at Hat Head. This store has rooms full of hats of all styles, shapes, and sizes. If you have a practical need, like a knit beanie to keep your ears warm when snowshoeing or a sun hat with neck cape for kayaking, it's here! Maybe Door County has you feeling all nautical, and you want a Greek fisherman's cap or a highfalutin captain's cap for selfies on the boat docks, they're here! Maybe you want something that expresses your unique personality, like a Breton cap for your '60s British rock band persona or an elegant cloche beret for . . . whatever you would wear that for, it's here!

And of course, there are baseball caps! Door County caps, sports teams' caps, Great Lakes–themed caps, funny caps, and more! So treat your head with a souvenir from Hat Head.

4075 WI-42, Fish Creek, 920-868-2371
doorcountyhats.com

DECORATE YOUR HOME
IN DOOR COUNTY–INSPIRED STYLE

Maybe you've fallen in love with the peninsula and decided to stake out a little piece to call your own. Lake house, condo, cabin, whatever it is, you're going to need furniture. Or perhaps you just want to find a signature piece to ship home, a lasting reminder of your time in Door County. Two unique home furnishings and accessory shops deliver exciting furniture and design.

Maxwell's House in Egg Harbor is brimming with eclectic high-design furniture and accessories in a vast array of styles. Furnish your whole house or find a cool unique piece to show off your style. Maxwell's House offers design services and welcomes professional designers.

Nathan Nichols in Baileys Harbor is a gorgeous showroom of classic and timeless furniture and accessories. The vignettes throughout the store are bursting with elegant lake-house vibes. Nathan Nichols also offers full design services or design consulting.

Maxwell's House
7763 WI-42, Egg Harbor, 920-868-2989
maxwellshousedc.com

Nathan Nichols
8068 WI-57, Baileys Harbor, 920-839-9779
nathan-nichols.com

TIP

Now that you're on the stylish home accessories hunt, be sure to stop at Blue Dolphin House and BDH Studio. Visit this exciting store and gallery, and you will return home inspired to infuse your home and your life with color and texture, from your earlobes to your tableware to your garden to the art on your walls. Blue Dolphin House features elegant, fun, and well-designed home goods, decor, and accessories. BDH Studio's galleries showcase exciting work from national and international artists including wall art, metalwork, textiles, and jewelry.

Blue Dolphin House and BDH Studio

10320 Water St., Ephraim, 920-854-4113
bluedolphinhouse.com

SHOP SCANDI

Al Johson's in Sister Bay is of course known for Swedish pancakes and goats on the roof. However, it also features two exceptional Scandinavian shops. The restaurant's official gift shop, Al's Butik, carries traditional Swedish items as well as clothing, purses, gifts, souvenirs, toys, goat-themed things, socks, candles, food items, and more! Skal features modern Scandinavian-designed home goods and accessories, including lots of items with Dala horses, as well as beach accessories, Swedish food, and gifts. Seriously, between the restaurant, the bar, Al's Butik, and Skal, you could make a vacation out of just a trip to Al Johnson's.

Want more Scandinavian shopping? Just up the road, Simply Scandinavian occupies a unique spot in the center of the Gills Rock marina. This little shop features Scandinavian-themed gifts and housewares, toys, kitchen gadgets, Dala horses, mittens, socks, and lots of fun stuff . . . and hedgehogs! Not live, but loads of hedgehog-themed items due to the shop's location on Hedgehog Harbor. (Fun side note: Look up Simply Scandinavian online for photos of it completely encased in ice!)

Al's Butik and Skal
Al Johnson's Swedish Restaurant & Butik
10698 N Bay Shore Dr., Sister Bay, 920-854-2626
aljohnsons.com

Simply Scandinavian
12743 WI-42, Gills Rock, 920-559-7803
facebook.com/SimplyScandinavianGiftShop

STOP THE CAR!
IT'S A FARM MARKET

Door County has many outstanding, fun, and eclectic farm markets and orchard stores. Be ready to pull off the road when one catches your eye. Below are popular markets to hit when you're out and about:

Koepsel's Farm Market is an iconic Door County farm market dating back to the 1950s that combines a fresh-food store, smoked-fish deli, and antique shop.

Wood Orchard Market has great products made from seasonal fruits and vegetables (like cherry horseradish sauce or apple donuts) in a family-friendly store featuring a pedal-cart track, playground, and frozen apple-cider pops for the kiddies.

Seaquist Orchards features orchard-grown cherry and apple products (like apple bourbon barbecue sauce or Bing cherry jam) and motor-coach tours through the orchards and working farm.

Bea's Ho-Made Products is a family business dating back four generations to the late 1800s offering homemade canned goods and specialty food products.

Koepsel's Farm Market
9669 WI-57, Bailey's Harbor
920-854-2433
koepsels.com

Seaquist Orchards
11482 WI-42, Sister Bay
920-854-4199
seaquistorchards.com

Wood Orchard Market
8112 WI-42, Egg Harbor
920-868-2334
woodorchardmarket.com

Bea's Ho-Made Products
763 WI-42, Ellison Bay
920-854-2268
beashomadeproducts.com

ACTIVITIES BY SEASON

WINTER

SPRING

SUMMER

FALL

SUGGESTED ITINERARIES

UNIQUELY DOOR COUNTY

GET OUTSIDE

NAUTICAL HISTORY

REVEL IN NATURE

CULTURAL IMMERSION

ART INDULGENCE

BE NOSTALGIC

FUN WITH KIDS

EXPLORE PENINSULA BREWS, WINES, AND SPIRITS

SUSTAINABILITY-FOCUSED TOURISM

Relax at one of Door County's many beaches

INDEX